LIFE, IS IT?

A TEEN'S GUIDE TO FIGURING THINGS OUT

AAMIR RAZA

Contents

Preface

Have you ever had those moments where you just pause and ask yourself, "What is this life?" I have. We all do, right? This book was born through those moments of reflection, the kind where you're just taking a breather from the chaos of everyday life.

It wasn't planned. It wasn't like I set out to write a book one day. I've always been into journaling and penning down my thoughts to dial the vortex of my brain down a bit. One fine day, it happened. Like life nudged me a little, and I started jotting down thoughts, experiences, and little reminders that helped me navigate life's ups and downs at that stage of my life where I was psyching myself up. Before I knew it, these reflections turned into chapters, and here we are.

My aim in writing this book is simple: to offer a familiar voice in the midst of life's uncertainties. It's an invitation to see life from different angles, to find magic in the mundane, and to remember that, even in the mess, there's something pretty incredible about just being alive.

This isn't a guide with all the answers. I'm just a teenager who has experienced enough of life's moments to give him a mental jolt, and yeah, figuring things out has led to a collection of musings, a bit of encouragement, and a reminder that we're all in this together, trying to figure things out one moment at a time.

So, whether you're feeling lost, inspired, or somewhere in between, I hope these words offer a bit of comfort, a spark of curiosity, and a gentle reminder to embrace the journey, whatever it may hold.

CHAPTER I

The Pause

Hey, you made it! You're here, right now, in this moment—how often do we think about that? The fact that we're alive. Breathing. Feeling. Thinking. Sometimes it all just *is*. But, have you ever taken an actual pause just to realize what a gift that is? And I'm not saying this in that cliché, preachy way, but really, amidst all your complaints about everything, do you realize how fortunate you are to live this moment right now? This exact moment, which will never return—how precious is that?

I mean, really, think about it. We get so caught up in the next thing, the next milestone, and the next big moment that we forget the small things that are happening *right now*. Knowing how short each moment of life truly is can bring a rare, placid sense of peace to our hearts. When we allow ourselves to fully experience and savor each moment, it becomes so much more than just a point in time—it's a gift, a precious reminder that we are alive in the here and now.

To fully experience life, it's vital to dive into each moment with curiosity and awe. Every moment is fleeting: no hour, minute, or second ever returns. So, why do we rush through life, oblivious to the beauty right in front of us? Truly relishing each moment offers a profound joy and brings a calm that grounds us. In a world that's often frantic and uncertain, learning to fully engage with the present is a rare and precious gift. The upcoming chapters will explore how we can weave this awareness into our lives, guiding us through the highs and lows as they come as life for all of us can go haywire in an instant.

But here's the thing: amidst all the chaos, the rush, the never-ending to-do lists, there's something magical happening. Right now, in this moment, your heart is beating, your lungs are filling with air, and your mind is racing with thoughts. We're blessed to experience all of this and to just be. Yet, how often do we stop to realize how fortunate we are?

A powerful tool to anchor us in the present is *mindfulness*. This practice allows us to tune into the world around us and extricate ourselves from unhelpful influences that clutter our minds.

When we're not actively engaged in something productive, it's essential to avoid drifting into pessimistic or meaningless distractions. In today's world, it can be especially challenging to steer clear of negativity, but being mindful of what we consume can make a world of difference. In today's age, where the temptation to veer into doom-scrolling or other such extraneous practices like incessantly binging on meaningless content is high, it takes all the more conscious effort to create mindful habits. Imagine swapping out those habits for time spent reading a great book, practicing gratitude, caring for yourself, or spending time with loved ones. These small, intentional actions sharpen our focus on what genuinely enriches our lives, sparing us from the negativity and distraction of unconscious routines.

It's natural to sometimes slip into memories of the past, to ponder over mistakes or things we wish had gone differently. Retrospection can be valuable for putting a finger on the patterns, drawing lessons from past experiences, and shaping a better future. Even so, there's a fine line between thoughtful reflection and dwelling on regret. Regrets are like chains that pull us back, stealing the peace of the present. Personally, I believe in letting go of regrets—once a moment has passed, it's beyond our reach, and what matters is how we choose to respond *now*. Obsessing over a future that hasn't arrived is equally damaging. Whether it's worrying about possible failures or living in daydreams of success, we risk missing out on what's right before us. As the saying goes, *"Don't let your past blackmail your present into ruining a beautiful future."*

Living a happier, more satisfied life is indeed within reach, but it's often the small, consistent actions—not grand gestures—that make a difference. Simple tweaks to daily routines, like getting enough sleep, taking regular exercise, or eating nourishing foods, set the foundation for a more joyful life. True satisfaction comes not from massive, huge leaps of changes but from nurturing small habits that align with our well-being. Boy, if you're taking pride in pushing through sleepless nights, neglecting your body, and working yourself to the bone without rest, thinking it's some badge of accomplishment—let me tell you, it's really not. To respect oneself is to listen to the body's needs and honor them. Sometimes, giving ourselves the basics—a full night's rest, a morning walk, a few moments of quiet—is all it takes to change the course of a day.

Together, we're going to look at life from different angles—shifting lenses to help you see that life is more than just the sum of its parts. It's a plethora of fleeting moments that, when pieced together, make up your journey. And trust me, there's so much magic in the here and now, if you just look for it. Plus, did you know that they call it 'the present' for a reason: it is life's rare offering, a moment served as a gift to learn from the past and shape a more thoughtful, purposeful future. Here, in the present, we are given the chance to evolve, amend, and set the course forward.

Moreover, this isn't going to be one of those deep, philosophical monologues or a complex breakdown of what life really is that makes your head spin. Nope. Toward the end of this journey, it'll be fitting to reflect on the title of this book. Life, is it? After all, in moments of despair, we often find ourselves grumbling, "What is this life? How did I end up with such a rotten fate?" And yet, during our most triumphant times, we declare, "I'm the luckiest person alive!" Life is truly an amalgam of different phases, each phase a chapter filled with its own lessons and meaning, be it dejection or sheer joy, a completely lazy mood where you'd rather not get up, a phase of loving to travel, a time of wanting nothing more than the comfort of home, or moments of desperation to experience thrilling adventure, or the enrapturing quiet times of stillness.. Life defies simple explanation, and yet, what an incredible, enigmatic gift it is—life, it is!

CHAPTER II

Alive and Overlooking It

I mean, think about it—we're human. Out of all the species on this planet, we get to live this incredible experience of *being.* Every intricate detail of our existence—the organs, tissues, cells working together—it's a miracle we're even here. We eat, we laugh, we cry, we connect with people who love us. Yet, somehow, we get so caught up in the noise, the drama, and the next big thing that we forget just how amazing it is to be alive.

Let's be real—life is messy. Disordered, to put it in a more suave and refined way. There's no script, no manual to follow, and certainly no guarantee that everything will go immaculate every day. You wake up, go through the motions, deal with whatever curveballs life throws your way, and repeat. Some days feel like you're killing it, while others, well, not so much. But here's the thing: that's okay—

We all have those days where it feels like the world is stacked against us. You know the ones—where nothing goes according to plan, and you feel stuck in a loop of frustration. It's enticing to throw in the towel and wallow in those negative vibes. In fact, the pull of negativity can be outlandishly tempting at times, right? There's a certain allure in embracing that melancholic mood, sinking deep into it, and thinking, "Well, this is just how it is." And hey, that's perfectly human.

Think about it this way: every day you have two choices. One option is to throw yourself into those negative thoughts—let them pull you down, wear a despondent and desolate face, and marinate in that heavy energy. It's easy to fall into that trap because it feels real in the moment. The bad days feel like they define who you are, like you're stuck there forever. The idea of digging yourself out seems exhausting. So why not just stay in it, right?

But there's the other option—what if you woke up and told yourself, "Yep, it's another day, and I'll do the best I can with what I've got." No pressure to win, no need to do everything perfectly, just a simple acknowledgment that it's okay not to have it all figured out. In your perspective, few people know it all is what it seems. However, it perhaps isn't true, and it isn't the way you believe it is. They might not know jack, so there you go—you don't need to follow someone else's playbook or match their rhythm. You do you. Keep doing what you love, even if some days you feel off your game. That's life. And isn't it refreshing to know that we don't have to be superhuman to make it work? It is totally normal and even better to let things be and work hard from your side. As that is all that's in your hands. For sure, time will speak for itself when you get the supreme results, and the world will see, for you would not need to blow the trumpet all around.

Now, let me be clear. I'm not saying we should ignore our emotions or pretend like life is always sunshine and rainbows. You are made sentient. There shall be days when everything feels heavy, and those emotions will try to take control. But the trick is not to let them drive the car. Have them sit on the passenger seat for a while, acknowledge too, but don't give them the keys.

Staying calm in the face of life's ups and downs is easier said than done, I know. Simply try to maintain your composure first by looking at the problem as one millionth problem of all the issues that are in queue in this mammoth series called life. What if we took things as they come, without getting too worked up in the need for control? Sometimes, life has a way of working itself out if we just give it the space to unfold. And yeah, that's definitely not the most uncomplicated and effortless task, but it's also kind of freeing. You don't need to have all the answers right now—you're alive, and that's enough.

Perspective often shapes our reality, especially when it comes to being alone. To some, solitude appears as loneliness—a void where thoughts spiral, self-doubt creeps in, and blame for imagined inadequacies festers. But solitude, when embraced, transforms into a sanctuary. It's a space to marvel at oneself, to rediscover the intricacies of existence, and to be in the beauty of simply being. Speaking from personal experience, there's an unparalleled charm in spending time alone. It's awe-inspiring how solitude offers a mirror to our inner world—a world we seldom pause to explore in the clamor of life. Whether one is deeply intellectual or delightfully eccentric, carving out moments of solitude becomes an exercise in extending time itself, where every second stretches into something more profound and cherished.

On another plane, there lies a subtle, esoteric bliss in simply acknowledging existence. Amid all our struggles, heartbreaks, and moments of despair, there is an undeniable magic in the fact that we are alive. Think about it—life, in its incomprehensible vastness, never ceases to whet our appetite for more. Yes, life is off-centered, often riddled with pain and the pursuit of fleeting pleasures, but it is also breathtakingly wholesome. To exist is to hold within ourselves the privilege of endless possibilities—to try, fail, dream, and rise again.

Perhaps the most crucial realization is this: Existence, per se, is a treasure too precious to be squandered in complaints. It's perpetually intriguing how, time and again, our ability to strive, live with our very own crafted panache, and finding meaning even in moments of disarray persists. In the art of cherishing life, it becomes evident that being alive is not just a state—it's an opportunity to infuse every moment with significance. Sometimes, that alone is enough.

Life is full of uncertainty, and we aren't the ones who make the rules. But we do have control over how we respond. So, maybe the next time a rough day hits, instead of sinking into that negative space, remind yourself that it's just one day. Keep doing what you love, even if it's messy or imperfect. And if all else fails, remember—you're alive. And that, in itself, is pretty incredible.

CHAPTER III

One Awkward Step at a Time

Talking about something we all face at some point—disappointment. A chapter life makes sure we don't skip. You've probably been there. You've put your heart into something, strived for it, put in all your hopes into it, presumably even dreamed about it. But it didn't happen, right? That feeling, when what you've been waiting for doesn't happen the way it was supposed to happen in your head—it stings. Maybe it was an opportunity that slipped away or a goal you didn't quite reach. But here's what I want to remind you: Life is *not* about that one possibility, or that one opportunity. It's about keeping yourself open to what's next.

See, failure? It's such an austere word, almost like a label stamping that you're not good enough. A label that reverberates with an almost punitive finality, erasing the effort it belies. This quintessentially brings down one's morale and looms as an unforgiving monolith. Yet, if one pauses to consider, perhaps the effort itself holds more significance than the label we attach to its result. You tried—poured your heart and soul into it—and that, above all, is what truly defines you. Outcomes, for all their weight, are but fleeting markers in a larger journey. This time, it may not have unfolded as hoped, but consider this: could it be that this wasn't your destination? That something greater, more aligned with your essence, waits on the horizon, unseen yet inevitable? Life often reroutes us not to deter but to guide us to where we're meant to be. Trust the process; trust yourself.

Think of it like standing at the edge of the ocean. Every wave that rolls in brings something new—seashells, bits of seaweed, tiny treasures washed ashore. We're often tempted to gather everything, holding tight to whatever we find, as if keeping it all will somehow make the experience more meaningful.

But here's the thing: the tide always pulls back. No matter how hard you try to grip those seashells, the waves will tug at them. The more you resist, the harder it is to stand steady. Letting go isn't about losing what the tide brings—it's about understanding that the ocean will always give and take. The beauty lies in what remains after each wave retreats.

Sometimes, we hold on to things—moments, people, worries—thinking they define us. But, just like the tide, life has its rhythm. When we let go and trust that another wave will come, we realize that what's meant to stay will settle naturally at our feet. Letting go isn't about loss; it's about making space for new treasures to wash ashore.

So, stand there, feel the water, and trust the ebb and flow. Letting go doesn't mean drifting away—it means flowing with the rhythm of life itself.

Here are a few steps, or rather, small shifts that will help us slowly but surely release the things holding us back:

i. <u>Letting Go of Romanticized Nostalgia</u>

We all have a tendency to look back and remember the past as something perfect. The friends, the events, the moments—each tinged with a rosy glow. Yet, when we really examine it, the past often wasn't as perfect as we remember. Letting go of this romanticized nostalgia is crucial for embracing the truth of what was. The messiness, the mistakes, the lessons—all of it shaped who we are today. Once we stop holding the past on a pedestal, we can appreciate it for what it truly was and step forward without the weight of false expectations.

v. <u>Releasing the Need for Applause</u>

Seeking validation feels natural, especially in a world that constantly rewards attention. But living for applause, for external validation, binds us to other people's perceptions. If we never hear the applause we crave, we're left empty. To let go of this need is to free ourselves from seeking approval and instead find fulfillment in our own actions. It's not about grand gestures or being seen—it's about the quiet, personal victories that define our purpose, even if no one notices them. These are the moments that shape us, far beyond the applause.

v. <u>Breaking Away From a 'Fix It' Mentality</u>

In a world where we are constantly told to solve problems and "fix" everything, it's difficult to accept that not everything can be mended. Relationships, people, and situations can remain broken in ways we never imagined. Letting go of this "fix it" mentality means recognizing that sometimes, the best course of action is not to fix but to accept. Life isn't always about putting the pieces back together; sometimes, it's about learning to live with the cracks.

v. <u>Shedding Habits That Define Identity</u>

Many of us define ourselves by the habits we've developed over time. Whether it's the routines, preferences, or roles we've taken on, we cling to these markers of identity because they feel familiar. But what happens when these habits no longer serve us? Letting go of them can feel like losing part of ourselves—but in reality, it's about making space for a truer, more authentic version of who we are. It's a chance to grow beyond the limits we've set for ourselves.

v. <u>Moving Past 'I Deserve Closure'</u>

We've all been there: chasing closure, searching for answers that will give us peace. But here's the truth—closure is often a myth. We wait for a neat ending to a messy story, thinking it will give us the resolution we crave. Letting go means accepting that not every chapter has a tidy conclusion. Sometimes, life leaves us in the middle of a story with no clear end, and that's okay. Letting go of the need for closure is about finding peace in the present, not in an imagined future where everything makes sense.

v. <u>Detaching From Overthinking 'What Ifs'</u>

The "what ifs" can be endless. "What if I'd said something differently?" "What if I'd taken a different path?" Overthinking these questions drains the energy we need to move forward. Letting go of the "what ifs" means accepting that the past is gone, and the only path that matters is the one we're on right now. Instead of replaying past decisions, we can focus our energy on the present moment, where true growth happens.

v. <u>Learning to Drop the Expert Facade</u>

In a world that values expertise and certainty, it's easy to fall into the trap of pretending we know everything. But that facade is exhausting and ultimately fruitless. Letting go of the need to be an expert allows us to reconnect with curiosity and humility. It opens the door to authentic growth and learning, reminding us that it's okay not to have all the answers. Embracing dubiety makes room for new possibilities.

v. <u>Letting Go of Future Fantasies</u>

Dreaming of an ideal future is a natural part of being human. But when those dreams become fantasies that we cling to, they can paralyze us. The perfect future doesn't exist unless we take steps toward it today. Letting go of future fantasies means shifting from waiting for a "someday" to living intentionally in the "now." It's not about giving up on dreams—it's about actively creating the life we want, step by awkward step.

v. <u>Unlearning the Need for Explanations</u>

Not every action or change in our lives requires an explanation. We often feel compelled to justify our choices to others, especially when they don't understand. Letting go of the need to explain ourselves is empowering. It's about trusting that our decisions are ours to make, and others' opinions don't define our worth. Sometimes, the best choice for us won't make sense to anyone else—and that's okay. It's their journey to understand, not ours.

v. <u>Liberating Yourself from Self-Appointed Roles</u>

Lastly, we often can't preclude the intrinsic urge to box ourselves into roles—"the responsible one," "the funny one," "the caretaker"—believing these labels define us. Letting go of these roles is about expanding who we allow ourselves to be. It doesn't mean abandoning responsibilities or neglecting others—it means freeing ourselves from the limitations of being only one thing. By shedding these roles, we open up the possibility to become more, to experience life more fully, and to let our true selves shine.

There's this one thing my mother has always told me that I absolutely cherish: *"If things go according to your plan, that's great. But if they don't, it's even better—it's God's plan."* It's a reminder to trust in the process, to have faith that life knows what it's doing, even when we don't. The more you let go of what you think *should* happen, the more you'll see the magic of what's actually meant for you.

So don't cling to that one missed opportunity. Let go, because life? It's always offering more than one shot. And as you step back and see the bigger picture, you'll realize—life isn't just about what you gain or lose. It's about embracing each moment, each twist and turn, and asking yourself with curiosity, *Life, is it?* This unpredictable journey is always evolving, and that's the beauty of it.

CHAPTER IV

Healing – Rising from the Ashes

Healing. Such a simple word to say, right? It rolls off the tongue with ease, often accompanied by well-meaning advice: "Just move on." But let's be honest. Is it ever that easy? If only it were a switch you could flip, erasing the pain, confusion, and weight of what's been. Healing is messy, nonlinear, and often feels like a war fought in the quiet corners of your own mind.

Have you ever found yourself replaying the same moments, over and over, like a broken record? Trying to rewrite the past or understand where it all went wrong? It's exhausting. But here's the truth: healing isn't about forgetting or even forgiving right away. It's a journey—one that takes time, patience, and, above all, kindness toward yourself.

You know who understands this perfectly? The phoenix. Yes, that mythical bird we've all heard about. It's not just a symbol; it's a lesson. Imagine burning yourself down to ashes—completely dismantling what was—only to rise again, more brilliant and resilient than before. The phoenix doesn't avoid the fire; it embraces it, knowing that transformation comes through it. We can be like that, too. When life breaks us down, we have the power to rise, stronger than ever. But let's not sugarcoat it: living in the ashes, that "in-between" phase, is excruciating. And it's okay to admit that.

The Ashes Phase

The ashes symbolize loss, grief, and confusion—those moments when you feel like everything has crumbled. It's the phase where people often say, "Just let it go," but letting go feels impossible. How do you move forward when the past clings to you like a shadow? The truth is, you don't have to move forward immediately. Sometimes, healing begins with simply sitting in the ashes, allowing yourself to feel the weight of it all. It's not weakness; it's humanity.

Flames of Transformation

The flames represent the struggle, the fight to rebuild. It's not a steady climb but a series of starts and stops. You'll stumble. You'll doubt yourself. But each small step forward—no matter how insignificant it seems—is a spark that keeps the fire alive. This is where courage comes in. Courage isn't the absence of fear; it's taking one more step despite the fear.

The Rebirth

Rebirth isn't about forgetting the pain or pretending it didn't happen. It's about integrating it into who you are—becoming wiser, kinder, and more aware. Healing doesn't mean you'll never hurt again; it means you've grown strong enough to face the hurt and keep moving forward. Like the phoenix, your scars become part of your beauty.

Setbacks Are Normal

Let's talk about setbacks. Healing is rarely linear. You might feel amazing one day and fall apart the next. That's okay. Progress isn't about perfection; it's about perseverance. Think of setbacks as part of the dance, not the end of it. These "practical" ways may help, but the real game-changer is understanding that only one person can truly guide you through this process—and that's you. When you're in the right mental space, you'll begin to heal more effectively. Let's now discuss how to create those conditions.

The Bigger Picture

Having a positive attitude doesn't mean pretending everything is fine when it's not. It means acknowledging your feelings but choosing not to dwell on them. It's about finding small moments of gratitude, even in the midst of pain. Bad days don't last forever, and neither do good ones. That's life's rhythm. Embrace it.

And when the noise in your head gets too loud? Take a step back. Breathe. Trust that life is unfolding exactly as it should, even if you don't understand it right now. You don't have to figure everything out today. You just have to keep going, moment by moment, step by step.

Healing isn't just about time passing; it's about what happens within that time. When going through hardships—be it emotional turmoil, personal setbacks, or even sickness—healing can feel like an uphill battle. There are days when exhaustion seeps into your bones, when even the simplest task feels monumental. People say, "You'll get through this," but in the moment, it doesn't always feel that way. Because when you're in the middle of it, healing isn't linear—it's messy, frustrating, and often slow.

But listen to this: your body, your mind, and your spirit are built for resilience. One of the most fascinating things I've come across is the way some parents instill this mindset in their children. There was a parent who gave their child a piggy bank—not empty, but with some money already inside. Every time the child faced an illness or a difficult phase, the parent encouraged them to be strong, reminding them that just as the piggy bank was already partially filled, he too had an inner reserve of strength. As the child slowly recovered, he was encouraged to add more to the piggy bank—just like building back his energy, his health, his willpower. When they finally got better, they'd use the saved-up money for something they wanted, a reminder that strength and patience always lead to rewards.

Healing works in a similar way. A strong mindset doesn't just help you cope—it physically influences recovery. Your body listens to your thoughts more than you realize. A mind filled with resilience, even in the face of pain, can shift the balance in your favor. When you believe in your ability to heal, you help your good cells take over the bad ones. Internal healing isn't just science; it's a belief system, a quiet yet powerful force working in your favor.

So while healing may feel like starting from ashes, remember this—ashes are proof that there was once a fire, and embers can still reignite.

CHAPTER V

The Rhythm of Emotions

Let's just put it out there: life isn't a straight path to happiness, and anyone claiming otherwise likely hasn't fully experienced the complexities and challenges of life or is conveniently skipping the messy bits. Emotions—raw, overwhelming, and sometimes confusing—are the essence of being human. They're not obstacles to overcome; they're experiences to experience.

Yet, somewhere along the way, society decided that certain emotions were "bad." Sadness is weakness, anger is destructive, and fear is embarrassing. But giving you a reality check: your emotions aren't good or bad. They simply are. They're signals, not failures. They don't define you but you define your emotions with the power to control them as and when required and sometimes not putting a control on them works and is in fact, the appropriate thing to do. Ignoring or burying them doesn't make them disappear; it only makes them harder to manage when they inevitably surface.

This chapter isn't about teaching you how to "fix" your emotions because there's nothing to fix. It's about understanding that emotions are part of the journey and learning to live with them—not despite them.

The Spectrum of Emotions

Imagine a color wheel where each shade blends into the next. That's how emotions work—interconnected, often overlapping, always evolving. Joy might sit opposite sadness, but they're not enemies. In fact, they depend on each other to exist. Without sadness, how would we truly appreciate joy? Without fear, would bravery mean anything?

Another way to think of emotions is as a musical scale. Every note contributes to the melody of your life. Some notes are soft and soothing; others are sharp and jarring. You can't create a masterpiece without both.

And yet, we often resist certain emotions. We try to avoid sadness, hide anger, and suppress fear. But suppressing emotions is like muting certain instruments in an orchestra—the result feels hollow. Every emotion, even the uncomfortable ones, has a role to play.

<u>Learning to Play Along</u>

Here's the tricky part: life doesn't always play the melody you expect. Sometimes it's a serene waltz; other times, it's a chaotic drum solo. And while you can't always control the rhythm, you can control how you respond.

Acknowledge Your Emotions: Suppressing emotions might work temporarily, but it's not a long-term solution. Ignored emotions have a way of resurfacing when you least expect it. Instead, try acknowledging them. Feeling sad? Sit with it. Feeling angry? Explore why. Emotions are signals; listening to them can reveal what you need.

Practice Self-Compassion: It's okay to not be okay. Seriously. You don't have to have it all together all the time. Be kind to yourself, especially on the tough days. Treat yourself like you'd treat a friend who's struggling—with patience and understanding.

Find Healthy Outlets: Emotions need expression. Talk to someone you trust, write in a journal, go for a run, or scream into a pillow if you need to. Letting emotions out in a healthy way prevents them from building up and overwhelming you later.

Remember the Big Picture: Life is bigger than any single moment or feeling. When emotions feel all-consuming, remind yourself that they're just one note in the symphony. They'll pass, and new notes will take their place.

Understanding Unsociable and Taciturn People

Not everyone expresses their emotions openly. Some people are quiet, reserved, or difficult to read. This doesn't mean they feel any less deeply. In fact, some of the most introverted people experience the richest inner lives. Trust me when I say this as I've been much of a taciturn myself;

There are countless reasons someone might seem unsociable or taciturn:

- They might be introverted, finding energy in solitude rather than social interactions.
- They could be over-stimulated, needing time to process their thoughts.
- Past experiences or traumas might make them cautious about opening up.
- Social anxiety might hold them back, even if they long to connect.

Whatever the reason, it's important to approach such people with empathy rather than judgment. Not everyone communicates in the same way, and that's okay. Sometimes, the quietest people have the loudest hearts—they just express themselves differently.

Finding Joy in the Impermanence

Here's a universal truth: nothing lasts forever. And while that might sound unsettling at first, it's actually one of life's greatest gifts. Impermanence is what makes moments precious. A sunset wouldn't be as beautiful if it lasted all night. Laughter wouldn't be as joyous if it never ended.

Life's impermanence applies to emotions, too. No matter how overwhelming a feeling might be, it's temporary. Sadness will pass. Anger will subside. Even joy, as wonderful as it is, will eventually make way for something else.

The key is to embrace this impermanence, to savor the good moments while they last and find meaning in the challenging ones. It's not about clinging to happiness or avoiding pain; it's about experiencing everything fully, knowing that it's all part of the journey.

Don't Compare Your Chapter 1 to Someone Else's Chapter 20

One of the greatest sources of emotional turmoil is comparison. It's easy to look at someone else's life and feel inadequate, especially in the age of social media. But here's the thing: everyone's journey is different.

You might be struggling with the basics while someone else seems to have everything figured out. But you don't know their full story. Maybe they've been through struggles you can't see. Maybe they're still struggling behind the scenes.

Life isn't a race or a competition. It's a personal journey, and comparing your beginning to someone else's middle or end is unfair—to you. Focus on your own path, your own growth. Celebrate your progress, no matter how small.

Real Talk

There have been days when my emotions felt like a storm—chaotic, relentless, and impossible to escape. Days when anger flared over nothing, or sadness weighed me down without reason. And there have been days of pure joy, when everything felt right, and I wished I could freeze time.

The truth is, I've learned just as much from the hard days as from the good ones. Maybe even more. Struggles have a way of teaching us resilience, of showing us our strength. They remind us that we're capable of enduring more than we think.

And no, I don't have it all figured out. None of us do. But that's the exquisiteness of life—it's a work in progress. Every emotion, every experience, every high and low adds to the masterpiece.

So, as you traverse your own symphony of emotions, remember this one line as I recollect jotting it in my diary, a couple of years ago:

"In the symphony of life, challenges are fleeting notes, but your resilience plays the enduring melody that prevails through every passage."

CHAPTER VI

In Good Times and Bad– Friends Not Fair-weather

Friendship, in its truest form, is not about numbers but about the depth of connection. A group of two or three loyal friends can often outweigh the appeal of a larger crowd. These are the ones who laugh with you, not at you—who might tease you in good humor but know when to stop. They'll pull your leg amidst trusted company but never let you feel belittled or humiliated. In a world where banter often masks veiled jabs, these friends stand out because their teasing is never a dagger disguised as wit.

The Art of Feeling Left Out (FOMO)

The art of feeling left out is a strange one, a sensation that twists in your tummy, making it uncomfortable to even breathe. Your tears hover at the edge, waiting to roll down from the canthi, yet you hold them back, resisting the urge to let them fall, determined to emerge stronger. It's when you're in a social gathering, surrounded by people who seem to be meshing perfectly with each other, and you're the one left on the outside, trying to fit in but never quite finding your place. You watch everyone else laugh, connect, and share moments, and it feels like the more you try, the further away you get. That feeling—the uncomfortable weight of not belonging—is a silent struggle that no one else seems to see.

Learning to escape this pain doesn't require forcing yourself to be someone you're not. It starts with accepting that it's okay not to fit in all the time. The moment you stop chasing every gathering, every conversation, and start cherishing the moments you do have, you begin to heal, not because you've found your place in the crowd, but because you've found peace in yourself. Sometimes, the best way to overcome FOMO is to give yourself permission to just be—not as part of a crowd, but as an individual who doesn't need anyone's validation to feel worthy. And in that stillness, you discover something profound: you are enough, just as you are.

The Subtle Red Flags

Here's something I swear by: _I can take a joke, but not when it's at my expense._ And believe me, there's a difference. Laughter is meant to unite, not isolate. When the joke crosses the line into mockery, it's no longer funny—it's a breach of respect. Of course, it's just as important to know how to take a joke. Life's too short to take everything seriously, and sometimes, a good laugh can be the best way to keep things light. But there's a difference between laughing with someone and laughing at someone—being able to tell that difference is key to keeping things fun without crossing the line. This distinction is crucial because disrespect in friendships often hides under the guise of "just kidding." But words, even those meant in jest, leave imprints. And the ones that sting linger far longer than anyone cares to admit.

That's when you begin to notice the subtle red flags—those little moments where a joke feels more like a jab than a friendly laugh. Have you ever laughed along with a joke about yourself, but deep inside, felt that uncomfortable twist in your stomach? It's the _"what am I, chopped liver?"_ moment—a silent plea to be acknowledged beyond the punch line. While humor is a foundation of many friendships, there's a fine line between being playful and being cruel. Insecure people, often wrestling with their own self-doubts, may use humor to elevate themselves at the expense of others. They think that by denigrating, even subtly, they shine brighter. But true friends don't derive their confidence from your discomfort. They know that your circle of trust isn't a ladder to climb—it's a circle to belong to.

When a person's words repeatedly leave you feeling sidelined, their actions might be speaking louder than any justifications they offer. There are no announcements, no grand gestures, just the quiet realization that the circle isn't as inclusive as you thought. And while it stings, it's also a cue to reflect on whether you're standing in a room that truly values your presence.

Real Friends, Real Conversations

True friends won't support you for your vices, nor will they let you down in public. Instead, they'll help you become cognizant of your shortcomings, not to judge or discourage you, but to encourage self-improvement. It's important for friends to be real with you—not so indifferent that they avoid addressing your flaws, nor so fake that they sugarcoat reality with hollow compliments. Friends who only flatter you without helping you face the truth are not companions of value—they're merely playing along in a façade that prevents growth.

A genuine friendship thrives on honesty. Real friends teach you when you're wrong and inspire you to change bad habits for the better, while still accepting you for who you are. They'll stand by you in loyalty, refraining from exposing your flaws to the world. Instead of disclosing your mistakes to a crowd, they'll guide you privately, ensuring your dignity remains intact.

Choosing friends who uphold these values is crucial. Look for those who encourage you to face your flaws and fix them, rather than those who merely bask in false glory alongside you. And as much as you should expect this from others, offer the same in return: inspire your friends to grow, but never lose sight of the importance of unconditional acceptance.

The Ache of Friendship Breakups

Furthermore, when the humor crosses that invisible line, it's often a symptom of something bigger—something deeper which is perhaps one of the most unspoken pains—the heartbreak of a friendship ending. Unlike other relationships, whose break-ups are often met with societal sympathy, the dissolution of a friendship often feels isolating. It hits differently when the people who were once your rock aren't there anymore. Whether through an argument or slow drift of someone you once told everything to—the one who knew all your secrets, your unspoken thoughts. The absence of someone who was once your closest confidant leaves a strange emptiness, realizing that the person who used to be your-everything is now a stranger to your life. That's the kind of loss that doesn't need words galore; it just leaves a quiet ache where they used to be. The grief is private, raw, and stretches across time, leaving a hollow where once there was joy. It's a phase that demands both time and emotional energy to heal. But these heartbreaks, as gut-wrenching as they are, teach us invaluable lessons. They remind us to be discerning, to treasure loyalty, and to recognize when a friend is truly a friend—not just a fair-weather companion.

The Beauty of Silent Support

There's something beautiful about the friends who don't need to speak much, but just show up. Like that one friend who, after a long, exhausting day, doesn't say a word but just sits next to you, maybe passes you a cup of tea, and doesn't ask you to explain yourself. It's the kind of comfort that doesn't need words, just their presence. I remember once, after a tough week, my friend just walked in, sat beside me, and we watched a movie without even discussing what was wrong. Sometimes, the loudest support is the quietest one. It's these friends who remind us that true companionship isn't always about solving problems, but simply being there through it all.

To offer my two cents, friends are like stars in the night sky. Some are bright, steady and guide you through dark times, while others flicker in and out, barely making an impression. But it's those steady ones—the ones that shine through even when the clouds roll in—that matter the most. The people you keep close shape your view of the world, just like stars influence the night sky. They can give you direction, comfort, and light when you need it most. And, just like stars, the ones who truly matter are the ones you can always count on to be there, even if you don't see them every day. Letting go isn't about being cynical; it's about protecting the balance in your life. It's about making space for those who enrich you, who'll stand by you—not just when the sun's out, but when the storm clouds gather.

When you find them, cherish them. Because ultimately, friendship isn't measured by the number of shared laughs or Instagram-worthy moments, but by the unspoken understanding in moments of silence. It's about knowing who will sit with you, no words needed, when life gets heavy. That's the kind of thread worth holding onto.

Your inner crew—it's not just about companionship or having someone to hang out with. Friends matter more than we often give them credit for. They're like mirrors and magnets at the same time. The people we surround ourselves with reflect a lot about who we are and, in many ways, shape who we become. Their habits rub off on us, their opinions influence our perspectives, and their energy either lifts us or pulls us down. Think about it—how many times have you caught yourself saying a phrase your best friend uses, picking up their quirks, or even reevaluating your decisions because of their input?

Friendship isn't just a feel-good part of life; it's a cornerstone of our mindset and growth. The right friends can inspire you, challenge you to be better, and keep you grounded. On the flip side, the wrong ones can derail your progress, breed insecurities, or lead you down paths you're better off avoiding. That's why who you choose to keep close isn't just a casual decision—it's a defining one. So, keep your circle small but mighty. Quality over quantity, always. Because in the end, it's not about how many people you know—it's about how many people really know you. When you find those rare, not-so-fair-weather friends, hold them close. They are the anchor in life's stormy seas, the constant in its chaos. And while they may not always make the loudest noise, their quiet presence often speaks volumes. Because at the heart of it all, friendship is not about perfection—it's about choosing to stay, in good times and bad.

CHAPTER VII

The Quiet Power of Generosity

Is the purpose of life merely to gain personal happiness and success, to achieve everything simply to please ourselves? How incongruous is this kind of life—gathering everything we can for ourselves and moving ahead alone? Or... could life mean something deeper, something more fulfilling, if we dared to shift our perspective?

We're all wired for it, I think. This constant chase. For more money, more stuff, more... well, more of everything. It's like we're on some endless treadmill, always striving, always wanting more. But honestly, does it really make us happier? We're constantly on the lookout for something that'll fill that space inside us, but does it ever really happen?

I've started to wonder if we're looking in the wrong place. Maybe, just maybe, true fulfillment doesn't come from hoarding everything for ourselves. Maybe it comes from... giving it away.

Hear me out. I know, I know. It sounds counterintuitive. But think about it. When was the last time you truly felt a sense of deep satisfaction, a real sense of purpose? Was it after you landed that big deal, or after you helped a friend in need?

Perhaps real happiness lies not in the hoarding of success but in spreading joy. Getting too absorbed in our own lives, our own needs, and our own ambition rarely leads to true contentment. Instead, when we choose to share with others, when we see generosity not as an act of charity but as an intrinsic part of living, we uncover a profound kind of bliss. For being kind ensues in providing solace, not just to the one you succor but to you as well. Come to think of it, 'being benevolent' is—not just helping someone or being of service, but doing so with a pure intent, without expectation or vanity. True generosity isn't about what we give or the size of our gesture. It's about doing it without being under duress, and without thinking of it as charity, but purely as a way to share joy and which ultimately culminates in finding you peace and balance.

In giving from the heart, we discover that it's not about the grandeur of our deeds but the purity of our motives. When we act with this kind of sincerity, we let go of the inner turpitude, the petty vices, and the self-centeredness that often clouds our vision. Just as it's said, no one has ever become poor by giving. Real wealth lies in the happiness, warmth, and connection we gain from uplifting others.

What we often fail to realize is that generosity can create a beautiful paradox—the more we give, the more we receive. It's a mystery, really. How can giving away our time, resources, or kindness possibly lead to more joy in our lives? But when we offer without reservation, without expectation, we create an energy that flows back to us, often in unexpected ways. Acts of kindness create ripples. They invite more kindness into the world and into our own lives, a positive feedback loop that can't help but grow. When you give generously, the world seems to reflect back that same generosity.

In today's world, where individualism reigns supreme and competition is often seen as the ultimate goal, it's easy to forget that generosity can be a revolutionary act. We're encouraged to hustle, to focus on "me," to strive for personal gain at all costs. But what if we disrupted this cycle? What if we stopped seeing others as competition and began to see them as opportunities for connection? Generosity challenges these norms and encourages a more compassionate, interconnected society. By giving—whether it's a smile, a compliment, or our time—we start to create bonds that defy the isolation and loneliness that can so easily be part of this fast-paced world.

Generosity is often seen as something grand or extraordinary. We might think of it as giving large sums of money or dedicating hours of our time to a cause. But sometimes, generosity is found in the smallest of moments—those seemingly insignificant actions that go unnoticed by the world. Holding the door open for someone, offering a sincere compliment, or taking the time to really listen to someone can have a profound effect. These small acts, though simple, are what ultimately build a compassionate society. They are proof that we don't need to make grand gestures to make a difference. The power lies in the consistency of these small, everyday actions. They accumulate over time, quietly shaping the kind of world we live in.

Interestingly, the very act of being generous can become a form of self-care. When we're caught in the whirlwind of our own stresses and anxieties, it's easy to get lost in our own minds, trapped in a loop of worries. But by focusing on others—by reaching out with kindness and understanding—we momentarily step outside of ourselves. We put our own struggles on pause and offer something of value to someone else. In these moments, we might find relief. The act of generosity brings a sense of purpose and fulfillment that can help soothe the turbulence inside us. It's a reminder that we're all connected, that our lives are intertwined, and that helping others can also help us heal.

Thus, maybe it's not about how much we achieve for ourselves but about how much we share with others. Each small, selfless act, done with a pure heart, brings us closer to a more peaceful, fulfilled life. Generosity asks us to look beyond personal gain and discover that real happiness has always been right here, waiting to be shared. Let kindness guide us, not as a grand act but as a quiet, steady way of living that brings both peace to us and light to the world around us.

Kindness, in its truest form, connects us to something bigger than ourselves. It's not about sacrificing our own well-being for the sake of others, but about finding fulfillment in making the world a better place, one small act at a time. By shifting our perspective—by choosing to live with generosity at the core—we can create a life of true contentment and peace. It's the quiet power of giving that often makes the loudest impact.

CHAPTER VIII

Forgives: A Heart That's Brave

A heavy heart, a wounded soul,
A silent pain, beyond control.

To forgive, to let go, it seems so hard,
A battle within, a weary guard.

But courage whispers, a gentle guide,
To break the chains, and open wide.

To mend the broken, and let love in,
To heal the wounds, and start again.

It takes strength, to face the bygone,
To let go of anger, to at last move on.

Extending forgiveness, a gift so rare,
A testament to love, beyond compare.

~Aamir

Forgiveness, a complex interplay of emotions and choices. It's a journey that demands courage, empathy, and a willingness to let go of the past. While offering an apology can be challenging, accepting one and forgiving the offender is often even more difficult.

<u>The Challenge of Offering an Apology</u>

Vanity, fear of rejection, and the discomfort of admitting wrongdoing can often hinder our ability to apologize sincerely. However, a genuine apology, delivered with humility and empathy, can mend broken relationships and foster deeper connections.

The Strength of Forgiveness

Forgiving someone who has hurt us deeply requires immense emotional strength. It's about releasing the negative emotions that hold us captive, choosing compassion over resentment, and embracing the power of letting go.

Bravery in Forgiveness and Acceptance

Accepting an apology is a courageous act. It involves vulnerability, trust, and a willingness to open our hearts to the possibility of healing. By choosing to forgive, we not only liberate ourselves from the pain of the past but also create space for love, understanding, and growth.

Not Every Grudge Should Be Avenged, Nor Every Wrong Forgiven

Forgiveness is a deeply personal journey. It's not something that can be measured by a universal rule, but rather something each of us must navigate with our own pace and intentions. It's tempting to believe that simply apologizing or saying "I forgive you" is enough, but the truth is that forgiveness requires far more. And let's be clear: forgiveness is not a blanket allowance to let go of every wrongdoing. Sometimes, there are mistakes too large, too severe to simply forgive with a wave of the hand, or else we'd be living in a world where jails, prisons, and justice systems wouldn't be necessary. After all, no criminal would ever be locked up if an apology could erase the consequences of their actions. But when done with the right intentions, when the heart is truly sincere, no parameter would be required to gauge the probity of that forgiveness—it's just known.

We must, however, approach forgiveness with our eyes wide open. It takes courage, and that courage comes from knowing what's right, not from being credulous or overly trusting to the point of blind acceptance. True forgiveness begins within ourselves, and to reach it, there are several steps we can take—each one tailored to our emotional readiness, our values, and the depth of the pain we are working to release.

Forgiving Oneself and Abandoning the "Colossal" Expectations

Forgiving others often feels like a monumental task, but forgiving oneself can be an even greater challenge. We tend to hold ourselves to impossibly high standards, replaying past mistakes in our minds as though punishing ourselves will somehow rewrite the story. This relentless self-criticism weighs heavily on our sense of self-worth, long after those we've wronged may have already moved on.

But self-forgiveness is not about letting ourselves off the hook. It's not an escape from accountability or a way to erase past actions. Rather, it's a recognition of our shared humanity—the understanding that to err is not just inevitable but a fundamental part of life. It's about owning up to our choices, learning from them, and using those lessons as stepping stones to growth.

Imagine, for instance, someone who speaks harshly to a close friend in a moment of frustration. They immediately regret their words, apologize sincerely, and their friend forgives them. Yet, days later, they find themselves replaying the scene, analyzing every word they said, and feeling consumed by guilt. Though the friend has already moved past it, the individual remains trapped, unable to extend the same compassion to themselves.

This inability to forgive oneself often stems from the misguided belief that holding onto guilt is a form of penance—a way to ensure we won't repeat the mistake. However, self-recrimination rarely leads to meaningful change. Instead, it drains emotional energy that could be directed toward healing and self-improvement.

To forgive oneself, the first step is acknowledgment. Accept the reality of the mistake without minimizing its impact or justifying it. Reflect on what went wrong and why, but also on what it taught you. Was it a lapse in judgment? A failure to communicate? Understanding the root cause is essential for growth.

Next, take action. Where possible, make amends to those affected. An apology or effort to rectify the harm done can be incredibly healing—not just for others, but for you. It signals a commitment to doing better and creates a pathway for closure.

Finally, let go. Understand that holding onto guilt doesn't serve you or anyone else. Treat yourself with the same kindness and patience you would offer to a loved one who made a mistake. Remember, self-forgiveness isn't about erasing the past; it's about choosing not to let it define your future.

As the saying goes, "Sometimes the hardest apology to accept is the one you owe yourself." This act of self-forgiveness liberates us, allowing us to move forward with renewed clarity and purpose. It reminds us that we are not the sum of our mistakes but the sum of how we grow beyond them. By forgiving ourselves, we reclaim our power—not to change the past, but to shape a better tomorrow.

One of the greatest burdens we carry is the unrealistic, colossal expectations we set for ourselves. Society, family, peers, and sometimes our inner critic urge us to excel in every domain, to never falter, and to always be perfect. These self-imposed standards, though motivating in moderation, often become nothing short of barbarous when weighed against our human capacity. With time, this relentless pressure spawns overthinking—a mental trap where every misstep feels like the end of the world.

Picture a student preparing for an exam. They set out with the determination to ace it, but the sheer weight of expectations begins to erode their confidence. The night before the test, they find themselves paralyzed, overthinking every possible scenario where they might fall short. Did they study enough? What if they blank out during the test? Instead of focusing on their preparation and trusting their effort, they spiral into self-doubt, convinced that failure is inevitable.

This barbaric cycle of expectation, overthinking, and self-recrimination leaves little room for growth or recovery. But here this thing: life rarely operates on a linear trajectory. Mistakes, wrong turns, and delays are not signs of failure—they're opportunities to course-correct, to pause and reassess, and to move forward with a new perspective.

Take, for instance, the analogy of Google Maps. When you're navigating to a destination and accidentally take the wrong turn, does the map go absolutely bonkers or berate you for your mistake? Does it freeze up in frustration or admonish you entirely? Of course not. It simply recalculates the route, calmly offering an alternative path to get you back on track.

Life, too, works in a similar fashion. One mistake—or even several—does not mean the end of the road. The map of our journey will always redirect us, offering new opportunities to reach our goals. But the key lies in acknowledging that missteps are inevitable and showing ourselves the same grace that Google Maps offers.

To do this, we must learn to be gentler with ourselves. We need to silence the inner echo that demands perfection and instead adopt an inner voice that says, "Don't fret; you can still work on it. There's always another way." Mistakes are not failures; they are proof that we are trying, learning, and growing.

This perspective doesn't absolve us of accountability. Rather, it allows us to frame our setbacks as stepping stones instead of roadblocks. Instead of obsessing over what went wrong, we can focus on what can still be done. It's a mindset that liberates us from the shackles of overthinking, reminding us that progress is more important than perfection.

Moreover, when we are kinder to ourselves, we create the mental space to reflect constructively. Instead of drowning in regret, we can identify what led to the misstep and how to approach it differently in the future. Just as a wrong turn on Google Maps can reveal an unexpected scenic route, our mistakes often lead to unforeseen opportunities or lessons that shape us for the better.

So, let's remind ourselves that we are human, not machines. There is no need to carry the crushing weight of impossible expectations on our shoulders. And when we falter, as we all inevitably do, let's choose to redirect rather than reproach. Life is not a race to be won but a journey to be navigated—with patience, resilience, and, above all, kindness toward ourselves.

By forgiving ourselves, we free our minds from the tyranny of overthinking. We learn to move forward with clarity and confidence, knowing that no single mistake has the power to define us. And just like the map that patiently recalculates our route, we can always find a way to move forward—no matter how far off course we might feel.

The Ultimate Intrepidity

It's a choice that requires both vulnerability and resilience. By choosing to bury the hatchet, we not only heal ourselves but also inspire others to do the same. It requires great courage to forward a hand of apology but an even greater deal of bravery to forgive and accept the apology.

the spellbinding days

A wistful ache often washes over me, a yearning for those days that shimmered with a golden hue. Those were the days—the days of our childhood that still have left us besotted, spellbinding—weren't they? If time machines existed, I wouldn't want to change a thing; I only have a yen to go back in time and feel that carefree joy again, to experience the world through the eyes of a child. I'd simply want to hop back and soak it all in.

Remember those carefree afternoons, don't you? The open sky above, a fresh breath of freedom, and our imaginations dancing in worlds only we could create. Before adulthood snuck in with its practicality and rules, life felt so wonderfully different. The skies were bluer, the grass greener, and every little moment was bursting with adventure. We, the boisterous little young'uns, found joy in the simplest of things—the soft rustle of autumn leaves beneath our tiny feet, the echoing laughter from a game of tag, the thrill of discovering a hidden creek in the woods.

It was as if we wore magic glasses, lenses that magnified the beauty in every detail. We saw the world with a clarity that vanished as we grew older. We noticed the intricate patterns in the clouds, the delicate dance of a butterfly, the way sunlight filtered through the leaves. We savored the taste of chilled lemonade on a hot day, the feeling of the wind in our hair, the pure joy of simply being alive.

Life was good back then, wasn't it? And guess what? It still is! Only that our perception of it has shifted. We've let the lenses get a tad murky, clouding our vision. So while we can't shrink back to those innocent days, we can definitely reclaim that purity of spirit.

We began life as a tabula rasa in childhood, in the most pristine form—untainted by the complexities of the world. In those early years, our charisma lay in the purity of our emotions, our unfiltered curiosity, and our ineluctable tendency to believe in the goodness of life. But as we grew, with each experience, the charm of that innocence evolved, shaped by the experiences, lessons, and trials we faced. While adopting a practical approach to life is necessary for survival in this world, it often changes how we observe and interpret life—no longer through a pure, untarnished lens but one tinged with caution, expectation, and even skepticism. Yet, even though we cannot return to that untouched state, it is vital to preserve the innate spirit of wonder and hope that once defined us.

Those were the days of blissful ignorance, weren't they? We didn't know the weight of responsibilities, the sting of rejection, the fear of failure. We existed in a state of pure potential, every day a blank canvas waiting to be filled with the vibrant hues of our imaginations. We were explorers, venturing into the unknown with fearless curiosity, our minds teeming with fantastical possibilities. We built elaborate forts out of blankets, transformed mundane objects into magical creatures, and believed in the existence of fairies and mythical beings.

The world was a grand adventure, a symphony of sights and sounds waiting to be discovered. We reveled in the simple joys – the warmth of sunshine on our faces, the taste of a freshly baked cookie, the feeling of sand between our toes. We were artists, poets, and philosophers, our lives a canvas of vibrant colors, our voices filled with unbridled joy.

Perhaps the most beautiful aspect of those days was the art of not knowing. We didn't overthink things, didn't worry about the future, and didn't try to control every outcome. We simply lived in the present moment, embracing the unexpected with open arms.

"Everything has its own time. We often make plans, we think we'll make very precise strategies, but even after all the attempts to execute them to the tee, life happens to be something totally different: what we plan and what actually happens, the time in between – that's life!"

Life, indeed, has its own way of unfolding. We can make plans, we can strive for control, but ultimately, it's the journey between the plan and the outcome that truly defines us. It's in those unexpected detours, those unplanned encounters, and those moments of serendipity that we discover the true essence of life.

Of course, childhood wasn't always sunshine and rainbows. There were tantrums, tears, and moments of frustration. But even amidst the chaos, there was a sense of wonder, a belief in the inherent goodness of the world. We trusted easily, loved unconditionally, and embraced every new experience with open arms. The ephemerality of everything nullified the infructuous petty issues. We didn't care to think or fret much about things unremittingly.

As we grew older, the world began to lose some of its magic. The innocence of childhood gave way to the complexities of adulthood – bills to pay, deadlines to meet, relationships to navigate. We learned about disappointment, heartbreak, and the harsh realities of the world. The world, once a playground of endless possibilities, began to feel more like a maze, filled with rules and limitations.

Things aren't quite the same anymore, albeit. The very nature of childhood itself feels more fragile now. You know that old saying, "It takes a village to raise a child?" These days, our village looks less like a Norman Rockwell painting and more like a sprawling, interconnected web. It's not just parents and teachers shaping kids anymore, is it? Now, we've got a world brimming with influences and the voices of young minds vying for validation: the allure of social media trends, the overnight rise of influencers, and, addressing the genuine, public figures who sometimes seem to be selling bravado disguised as wisdom. What's disturbing is how casually these ideas, some of them far too grim, are being tossed out to viewers as if they're harmless entertainment.

It's a strange new world, and it's unsettling how easily these influences can take root. Children, with their minds like fresh clay, absorb everything around them, the good and the bad, often without the critical filters that come with age. And with the digital world offering 24/7 access, often in the privacy of their own rooms, it's an avenue where careful guidance is more crucial than ever. You see a lucid twisted narrative that tells young minds that aggression equals power, that cruelty is cleverness, and that respect is something to be demanded rather than earned. It's not always about one bad influence either and rather it's the collective noise. The casual remarks that mock certain groups, and the glamorization of reckless behavior. And yeah, it culminated all to reap the expected menacing results. We see the effects, don't we? It's not just the casual profanity that might make us wince, or the way aggression can be normalized in online exchanges. It's the insidious way certain ideas, to name a few, the subtle misogyny, a warped sense of power, the "might makes right" mentality—are being packaged and sold to young minds.

I'm not interested in simply pointing fingers. This isn't about some generational blame game. But we have to be real: these things don't materialize out of thin air. They accumulate, bit by bit, in the content kids consume, the interactions they witness, the values (or lack thereof) that are modeled for them. The danger lies in young people being shaped by forces they don't yet understand. This isn't just a parental burden. It falls on all of us: educators, content creators, society as a whole. We can't afford to be passive, hoping kids will somehow navigate this minefield unscathed. We need to actively cultivate environments where kindness is valued, where respect is foundational, and where a healthy sense of self-worth isn't built on tearing others down.

And let's be clear, this isn't about helicopter parenting or stifling curiosity. It's about being present, engaged, and offering guidance that helps young people develop their own moral compass. It's about fostering critical thinking, so they can discern between genuine role models and those who offer only a hollow imitation. Sometimes, it's as simple as having open conversations, providing a counter-narrative, and living our own lives in a way that models the values we want to instill.

It's a complex challenge, yes. But it's also a profound opportunity. We have the chance to shape a generation that's not only informed but also compassionate, resilient, and grounded in empathy. And that's a village worth building, wouldn't you agree?

But amidst the chaos and the complexities, the spark of that childhood wonder still flickers within us. It's in the way we marvel at a breathtaking sunset, the way we get lost in a good book, the way we feel a surge of joy when we witness something truly beautiful. It's in our capacity for empathy, for compassion, for believing in the goodness of humanity.

We can't return to those carefree days, but we can reclaim that spirit. We can choose to see the world with fresh eyes, to embrace the unknown with curiosity, to find joy in the simple things. We can cultivate gratitude for the present moment, for the beauty that surrounds us every day. We can nurture our inner child, the part of us that still believes in magic.

This is the true gift of childhood – not just the memories themselves, but the lessons they hold. They remind us of the importance of joy, of the power of imagination, of the beauty of simply being alive. They inspire us to live with more intention, to embrace the present moment, and to find wonder in the everyday.

By rediscovering that childlike sense of wonder, we can enrich our lives in profound ways. We can reconnect with our inner selves, cultivate deeper relationships, and find a renewed sense of purpose and meaning. We can learn to live more fully, more authentically, more joyfully.

The journey of life is not always easy, but it can be truly magical. And the key to unlocking that magic lies within, in the echoes of our childhood, in the whispers of that inner child who still yearns to explore, to discover, to dream.

It's a faded photograph—one's tender years; a whisper on the wind. We chase the ghost of it, trying to recapture that feeling, that magic. But the fact is, it's not about going back. It's about finding the echoes of that child within—the whispers of wonder that still linger beneath the surface. The gap between the child we were and the adult we've become? That's where the real adventure lies. It's a space of rediscovery, of reawakening the senses, of embracing the unknown with the same fearless curiosity we once possessed. I remember how blithe my childhood was—playing the silliest of games with my cousin brother and my siblings. We'd have a ball each day, getting delirious over an extra hour of our favorite cartoon or T.V. show or perhaps a long bike ride, or simply to head outside and have thrill over in the swings. Time seemed endless. We'd have so much fun, sometimes a little too much that consequently we used to get reprimanded by our parents but then, next day, a new chapter begins. We forget what happened the previous day and just were in the moment. The time spent in school too, was nothing short of a treasure, something I'll fondly cherish forever. I was, admittedly, a teacher's favorite (chuckles). It was there that my interest in intellectual pursuits, passion for performing arts, and skill in public speaking first took root and flourished. Now, all that is sealed within a term coined as nostalgia by others, but for us, it's something inexplicable. For me, it was—and still is—the happiest time of all.

CHAPTER X

Do We Really Care?

Another question—have you ever been in a place where you're just way too exasperated with certain things, or even certain people? Maybe they've been showing off a bit too much attitude, or they got something you feel you deserve to have had. Or maybe, they've pulled some sneaky tactics, or worse? Just to add, let's not forget the ones who've become all supercilious overnight. Sound familiar?

Yeah, everyone's been there. What about you? Oh, don't pretend like you haven't! We've all been there, right? It's like, you're thinking about someone, wondering why things worked out for them the way they did, or maybe you're frustrated because you could've been in their shoes but somehow didn't make it there. Life happened, right? Sometimes it just doesn't work out, and sometimes it wasn't even meant to. But here's something we don't always remember—those people, the ones you think have it all together, have their own set of issues and shortcomings to deal with. Just because we see the snazzy, polished side of their lives doesn't mean they're the happiest people in the room.

Yeah, it's easier to preach than to practice, no doubt. But can't we, just for a moment, stop and think about what we're doing? Maybe the real focus should be on what we're creating and how we're excelling at it. The goal isn't about the final result or the glitzy outcomes we believe others are achieving. It's about the honesty and hard work we put into whatever we're doing. We've all heard the phrase "the grass is greener on the other side," right? And maybe it is greener, but why are we stepping away from our own green patches to obsess over someone else's?

The truth is, when you channel your energy into things that aren't really worth it, you lose sight of the good things in your own life. You dwell, you overthink, and meanwhile, the people you're stressing about? They're just living their lives, unbothered, as they should be. The only thing that changes is you being hard on yourself, beating yourself up for no reason.

Let's delve deeper into this "beating ourselves up" part. Often, our frustration with others stems from our own insecurities and unmet needs. When we see someone else succeed in a way we feel we should have, it can trigger feelings of inadequacy and self-doubt. Instead of acknowledging their accomplishments and seeking to understand how they achieved them, we might resort to downplaying their efforts or even resorting to petty criticisms.

In today's social media-driven world, the pressure to compare ourselves to others is stronger than ever. We scroll through posts showcasing someone's perfect vacation, their career success, or their seemingly flawless lifestyle, and it's easy to feel like we're falling behind. You've probably seen that one friend who posts every achievement—whether it's a new job, a fitness milestone, or an enviable social circle. It's natural to wonder, "Why aren't I there yet?" or feel frustrated by your own progress. But here's the thing: what we see online is only a curated version of someone's life. Just because their feed looks perfect doesn't mean their reality is. It's easy to forget that everyone, no matter how polished their profile, faces struggles and insecurities behind the screen. When we let ourselves get caught in the comparison game, we waste valuable energy focusing on someone else's journey rather than our own. Instead of envying their highlight reel, why not turn the lens inward? Focus on your own growth, celebrate your wins, no matter how small, and stay committed to what matters most to you. Social media can be a distraction, but your life is the one worth investing in.

Imagine, for instance, encountering a colleague who has recently been promoted. Instead of applauding their success and humbly inquiring about their journey – perhaps they developed a crucial new skill, worked tirelessly on a challenging project, or cultivated strong relationships within the company – we might find ourselves dwelling on our own perceived shortcomings, wondering what we did wrong or why we weren't chosen instead. This negative self-talk not only hinders our own growth but also prevents us from learning from others' successes.

It's crucial to remember that success often comes from a combination of hard work, dedication, and a unique set of skills and circumstances. While we might not possess the exact same talents or opportunities as others, we can always strive to improve ourselves and learn from their experiences.

Furthermore, focusing on others' perceived shortcomings can be a distraction from our own journey. When we constantly compare ourselves to others, we lose sight of our own strengths, goals, and aspirations. We become entangled in a web of negativity, wasting precious energy and mental bandwidth on things outside our control.

So, here's the thing: build your confidence, silently, like a tiger stalking its prey. Focus on making things happen in your own lane. When the world is chasing after loud, dazzling success, you can find fulfillment in perfecting the tiny things. Because in the end, those are the things that truly matter.

And as for the people who've been impudent, here's the kicker: trust that life has a way of balancing things out. People who throw shade or act poorly often end up facing their own consequences, whether they realize it or not. Just give it time. Everyone has their own timeline; their day in the sun will come, just like yours will.

Can we focus on doing our own thing and keep our eyes on our own path and let the universe handle the rest, I believe certainly. While they're busy playing games, you're busy building something real. Let their actions slide off your back, because the best revenge is simply living your life well.

So, do we really care? Sure, we all have those moments of frustration, but at the end of the day, we do not want to waste energy worrying about others when we could be pouring that same energy into our own growth? Life's too short to be sidetracked by the drama of certain pompous windbags.

Let's keep it simple: focus on your journey, embrace your quirks, and celebrate your wins—no matter how small. Because in the grand scheme of things, what truly matters is how you show up for yourself. So the next time you find yourself worked up in someone else's narrative, just remember: your story is the one you're writing, and it deserves all your attention.

And honestly? If people want to play games, let them. As for me, I show up with a blasé attitude that manifests effortlessly, without any contrived effort. Likewise, you've got a life to live—so go out there and make it spectacular!

CHAPTER XI

Innate Striving—No Plug Needed

If we're being honest, motivation can feel like a fickle friend. One minute, you're on fire—crushing your goals, knocking tasks off your to-do list—and the next, you're staring blankly at the ceiling, wondering, "Why even bother?" It's frustrating, isn't it? Like trying to catch a butterfly with your bare hands: one second it's there, the next, it's gone. But here's the thing—what if motivation didn't have to be so unpredictable? What if there was a way to create a steady, reliable source of drive that didn't depend on rewards or external praise? What if you could rely on something that didn't need to be plugged in, recharged, or boosted by others?

That's where intrinsic motivation comes in. This kind of motivation comes from within—doing things because you enjoy them, because they're meaningful, because they align with your values, not because you're chasing an external reward or recognition. Think about it this way: you don't run because you want a medal (although that's nice); you run because it feels good, because it challenges you, because it brings you peace. Intrinsic motivation is the engine that keeps you going, not because someone's watching or because there's something to win, but because it's simply you.

And here's the cool part: intrinsic motivation is more than just a nice feeling. It leads to persistence. When you're intrinsically motivated, you're more likely to stick with something, even when it gets tough. You're more likely to be creative, more open to learning, and just generally more engaged. And let's not forget the psychological perks—when you're doing something you're intrinsically motivated to do, your brain actually lights up in ways that make you feel happier and more fulfilled.

So how do we tap into this magic, and how do we keep it from feeling like a fleeting spark? First, it starts with figuring out what you really care about—the things that truly matter to you. What brings you joy? What makes you lose track of time? These are the activities that can fuel your motivation in the long run. It's not about checking off a to-do list; it's about diving into things that give you a sense of purpose and fulfillment.

Once you've figured that out, setting goals becomes a lot easier. But here's the twist—make sure your goals are aligned with what matters to you, not with someone else's expectations or standards. It's easy to get caught up in chasing after things that look good on paper or that society deems important. But when your goals are tied to your own values, they become something that drives you from the inside out.

Another way to nurture intrinsic motivation is to focus on the process, not just the end result. Sure, it's awesome to achieve a goal, but the real magic happens during the journey. Whether it's learning a new skill, experimenting with an idea, or simply enjoying the flow of an activity, the process is where you'll find joy. When you love what you're doing, the outcome doesn't feel like the only prize—it's just the cherry on top.

Speaking without sugarcoat things—life's never in a perpetual-smooth sailing mode, and that's okay. Setbacks are part of the ride. The key is to see them as opportunities for growth rather than roadblocks. If you trip up, don't beat yourself up. Learn from it. Every mistake is a chance to get better, to figure out a new way forward. And speaking of being kind to yourself—self-compassion is huge. When you slip up, be gentle with yourself. It's easy to get frustrated when things don't go as planned, but beating yourself up only drains your motivation. Treat yourself like you would treat a friend, and that friend is likely to bounce back stronger.

External pressures, yeah that's a big one. We live in a world that loves to tell us what we should want, how we should act, and where we should be by a certain age. Society's expectations can be loud, and they can make us feel like we're constantly chasing something we don't even care about. Whether it's the pressure to have a certain career, to live up to someone else's standards of success, or to always be "doing" something, these pressures can chip away at your motivation, making you lose sight of what truly drives you.

The key here is to tune out the noise. Not everyone's opinion matters, and not every expectation is worth living up to. When you're rooted in your values and your passions, you can start to recognize which pressures are worth listening to and which are just distractions. It's okay to say no to things that don't align with who you are. Sometimes, it takes getting comfortable with the idea that not everyone will approve of your choices. But when you're living authentically, you'll feel a deeper sense of fulfillment than any external reward could ever provide.

In addition to this, creating an environment that fosters intrinsic motivation is just as important as tapping into it. You don't need external pressures—forget about chasing rewards, promotions, or constant validation. These things can motivate us temporarily, but true, lasting motivation comes from within. That's why it's important to minimize the distractions that pull you away from what you really care about and focus on giving yourself the freedom to pursue things that feel meaningful to you.

Autonomy is a big player here. The more control you have over your actions, the more motivated you'll feel. When you're able to choose what you want to work on, when you can make your own decisions, you'll naturally feel more engaged in the process. That's why it's essential to surround yourself with people who support your goals, cheer you on, and remind you of why you're doing what you're doing. A good support system can be like rocket fuel for your motivation.

But let's be real: it's not always easy. Perfectionism can be a huge roadblock. Waiting for things to be just right before you act is one of the quickest ways to kill your motivation. Mistakes are part of the process, and they don't make you a failure—they make you human. Strive for progress, not perfection. And if you find yourself procrastinating or getting distracted, focus on breaking things down into smaller, more manageable steps. Tackling one small thing at a time can make a big project feel less overwhelming.

And hey, burnout is a thing. It happens when you push too hard, too fast, without taking the time to rest. Don't neglect self-care. You need time to recharge, to refresh your mind and body. When you take care of yourself, motivation comes easier, and it lasts longer.

Lastly, mindfulness can help you stay connected to your intrinsic motivation. It's easy to get caught up in the noise of external pressures, but when you take the time to check in with yourself and stay present, you'll find that your internal drive becomes clearer and more focused. It's all about balance—understanding what motivates you, honoring that motivation, and embracing it without needing an external plug-in.

The bottom line? Intrinsic motivation is the real deal. It's not something you need to chase or plug into—it's something that comes from within. When you align with your values, focus on the journey, and embrace challenges, you build a wellspring of motivation that can carry you through even the toughest days. So, what's the one thing that excites you for the pure joy of it, not for the applause at the end? Dive into it. Pursue it with passion, with purpose, and with the confidence that the drive to succeed is already within you. There's no need for external fuel. Just your own strength, your own will to push forward, is all you need. And you'll see that the next time you feel your motivation slipping away, a voice ensues to remind: *you've got this.* The strength you need to keep going is already inside you—you just have to tap into it.

CHAPTER XII

Building Confidence—It's Child's Play?

Let's dive right in: confidence. For some, it feels like a second skin, but for others, stepping into the spotlight can be as daunting as climbing a mountain. I understand. Making new friends? Talking to strangers? Or even facing a crowd to speak? It can be tough! But what my mind says is that if one lets their inhibitions go, it can become as easy as child's play.

I've always been passionate about communication, and my journey with elocution has been a significant part of my personal growth. I vividly remember those initial nerves, the trembling hands, and the butterflies in my stomach before stepping onto the stage. But with each performance, I learned to excel the challenge, to find my voice, and to connect with my audience on a deeper level. This has made me happy in so many ways. I found myself drawn to theatre, monologues and so many other events too.

Having seen it countless times – people's voices trembling, hands shaking, and faces turning red as they confront their fears. And you know what? That's perfectly okay for a beginner. Why does your voice shake? It's simple: when you're nervous, your body goes into overdrive, and that excess adrenaline floods your system as it prepares for a fight-or-flight situation. So, if you find yourself feeling jittery, remember: you're not alone in this!

But here's where it gets interesting. To help get rid of that excess adrenaline, I've found that many speakers, myself included, do a little warm-up backstage – maybe a quick jog or some jumping jacks to get the blood flowing. It sounds silly, but trust me, it helps! Deep breathing is also a game changer. Inhale deeply, hold it for a moment, then exhale slowly. It's all about calming those nerves and reminding your body that you're alright.

<u>A Deeper Dive into Insecurities</u>

Now, let's take a moment to talk about those insecurities that often creep in, especially when you're standing in front of others. Fear of judgment, self-doubt, or even imposter syndrome can sneak up on the best of us.

Let's start with the fear of judgment. We all know that feeling of imagining the worst-case scenario – thinking that if we mess up, everyone will notice and judge us. And more often than not, that fear is a product of our own imagination. The truth is, most people are too busy worrying about their own insecurities to scrutinize yours. When we're nervous, we tend to exaggerate what we think others might be thinking about us. But in reality, people are usually more forgiving than we give them credit for.

Then there's imposter syndrome. It's that nagging feeling that you don't belong, even when you do. It can happen in any situation, whether it's public speaking, at work, or in social settings. You might think, "Who am I to be here? I don't deserve this." But here's where it all comes to make sense: everyone feels this way at some point! The key is to recognize it for what it is – self-doubt – and challenge it. Remind yourself that you belong and that your experiences and skills are valid.

To tackle these apprehensions, it's essential to challenge those negative thoughts. The next time you feel insecure about speaking or putting yourself out there, ask yourself: Is this thought based on fact or fear? More often than not, you'll find that it's just the fear talking. The best way to deal with negative thoughts is to replace them with more empowering ones. Instead of thinking, "I'm going to mess up," try, "I am prepared and capable." Over time, these new, positive thoughts will become your default mindset.

<u>Building Confidence in Everyday Life</u>

Confidence doesn't just play a role in public speaking – it's crucial in every part of life. Whether it's making new associates, advancing in your calling, or navigating personal relationships, confidence is what empowers us to act boldly.

Start by setting small, achievable goals. If you want to speak up more in meetings or have more conversations with strangers, make it a point to take one small action every day. Don't be afraid to sound brazen. Maybe it's as simple as saying hello to someone new at work or offering an idea during a group discussion. Each time you step out of your comfort zone, no matter how small the action, you're building confidence.

Another powerful way to build confidence is by celebrating your wins. It doesn't matter how small the success – acknowledge it. If you managed to have a difficult conversation with a friend or speak up in a meeting, take a moment to recognize that achievement. These small victories add up over time and make you feel more capable.

Surround yourself with supportive people who encourage you to take risks and build your confidence. Sometimes, we need external reinforcement to remind us of our strengths. Whether it's a mentor, a friend, or a supportive colleague, having people who believe in you can make a world of difference.

<u>The Power of Vulnerability</u>

There's something powerful about vulnerability. In a world where perfection is often the goal, accepting our vulnerabilities can actually be a strength. When we allow ourselves to be open and authentic, we invite others to do the same. This creates honest connections that go beyond surface-level interactions.

Sharing personal experiences, even the imperfect ones, can help build trust with others. Whether it's acknowledging a mistake or sharing a vulnerable moment, these actions make us more relatable and approachable. Think about the most inspiring speakers or leaders you admire – they often share their struggles, fears, and failures, making them human and real.

Vulnerability also creates a sense of belonging. It tells others, "I'm not picture-perfect, and that's okay." And when we express our true selves, we open up the opportunity for others to do the same, creating a cycle of trust and respect.

Finding Your Voice

Discovering and developing your unique voice is key to becoming a confident communicator. Your voice is a reflection of your identity, beliefs, and values, and it's something that no one else can replicate. The more you get in touch with who you are, the more authentic your communication will be.

Start by reflecting on what matters most to you. What are your passions? What do you stand for? The clearer you are about your own values, the stronger your voice will be. This is especially important when it comes to public speaking or any form of communication. When you speak from a place of authenticity, your words carry more weight and meaning.

A great way to find your voice is by practicing – whether it's journaling, speaking in front of a mirror, or talking with trusted friends. As you practice, you'll start to get a sense of how you naturally express yourself and how to bring your unique perspective into your communication.

Real-World Examples and Case Studies

Let's look at some real-world examples of people who overcame their fears to make a significant impact. Take Maya Angelou, for example. Despite being a renowned writer and speaker, Angelou once admitted that she was terrified of speaking in front of people. But over time, she learned to embrace her voice and speak with such authenticity that she became one of the most respected figures in the world of literature and public speaking.

Another example is Steve Jobs, who was famously nervous about public speaking in the early days of his career. But by practicing and pushing through his fears, he became a masterful communicator, delivering some of the most impactful keynote speeches in history.

These examples show that even the most successful people had to face their insecurities and overcome their fears to find their voice. If they can do it, so can you!

Accordingly, as we wrap up this chapter, I want to leave you with this: confidence isn't something we have to build from scratch; it's already within us. Often, though, it gets tucked away behind the doors of our insecurities, and we end up feeling paranoid about stepping out.

Believe me when I say take a moment to calm yourself. When you do, you'll likely find that those hidden reserves of confidence are ready to shine. Note that confidence is not something that we either have or we don't - it can be developed and strengthened over time. Remember, it's all about taking that first step, trusting in your abilities, and allowing your voice to be heard.

Life is too short to let insecurities hold you back. Embrace the process, be gentle with yourself, and see where it takes you. Speaking from the heart isn't just a skill; it's a gift we all have, waiting to be shared. So, go ahead – let your confidence flow, and watch how everything else falls into place. After all, life is about accepting every opportunity to express yourself, so why not start now?

CHAPTER XIII

The Odyssey of Learning – Moving with Meaning

Life seems a lot like a tumultuous river. You see, it rushes forward, carrying us along on its capricious currents. We navigate its rapids, sometimes effortlessly, sometimes clinging to the rocks, always learning and evolving. Along this journey, we encounter a myriad of experiences, some joyful, some challenging, all of them contributing to the uniqueness of our lives. These experiences, like the pebbles in the riverbed, shape the very course of our journey, influencing our perspectives, our values, and ultimately, who we become.

<u>Navigating the Rapids</u>

I vividly recall the day I received news of the passing of a close relative. The joy I had been experiencing just hours before – a successful milestone at my academic life – felt abruptly muted, a stark contrast to the wave of grief that washed over me. It was as if the vibrant colors of my day had been suddenly drained, replaced by a somber gray. This experience taught me that life's emotions are often intertwined, a complex symphony of joy and sorrow, a delicate dance between light and shadow. It taught me that resilience lies not in denying or suppressing difficult emotions, but in acknowledging them, honoring them, and finding ways to navigate through the turbulent waters.

Grief, in its profound depth, challenged me to re-evaluate my priorities. It forced me to confront the fleeting nature of time and the importance of cherishing the moments we share with loved ones. I spent more time with family, savoring simple conversations, listening intently to their stories, and appreciating the unique bond we shared. I learned to appreciate the simple joys of life more deeply, to find solace in the memories we had created together, and to cultivate a deeper sense of gratitude for the time we have been given. This experience, though deeply painful, ultimately strengthened my resolve to live a life of purpose and meaning, to make the most of every moment, and to cherish the connections that enrich our lives.

Unburdening the Soul

For a long time, I carried the weight of a past hurt, like a heavy cloak of thorns, its sharp points digging into my soul, leaving me feeling drained and isolated. Holding onto grudges is like carrying extra baggage. It weighs you down and makes it hard to put your mind into something else. I remember holding onto a rancor against a former friend, replaying the hurtful memories in my mind like a broken record. It took a toll on me emotionally and socially. It certainly had left me feeling betrayed and resentful. As I replayed the memories in my mind, each time the anger and hurt intensifying, leaving me feeling like I was drowning in a sea of negativity. The memory felt like a phantom limb, a constant, aching reminder of the pain I had endured.

The resentment I harbored not only poisoned my relationship with my friend but also cast a shadow over my other relationships. I found myself withdrawing from social situations, fearing similar betrayals. I carried this emotional baggage with me everywhere, a constant weight on my shoulders, hindering my ability to fully engage with the present moment. Joy felt muted, laughter seemed distant, and the vibrant colors of life seemed to fade.

One evening, I found myself confiding in Mom about the lingering hurt I was carrying. As I poured my heart out, sharing the details of the incident and the ongoing emotional turmoil, I felt a sense of relief wash over me. Mom, ever the wise and compassionate listener, gently placed her hand on mine. She sat quietly, her gaze unwavering, offering a safe space for me to express my emotions.

I was hesitant to share my feelings, fearing judgment, but as I spoke, a wave of relief washed over me, as if a heavy weight had been lifted. Mom reminded me of my own resilience, of my ability to overcome challenges, and of the importance of self-compassion. She gently suggested, 'Perhaps you're holding onto this anger more for yourself than for your friend.' Her words resonated deeply. I realized that holding onto this anger wasn't having an effect on my friend in any respect, rather it was hurting me more than I realized. It was preventing me from experiencing true joy and limiting my ability to build meaningful connections.

That conversation with Mom was a turning point. It opened a space for me to acknowledge the hurt I had experienced, to validate my emotions, and to treat myself with the same kindness and understanding that I would offer a friend in need. I began to see that forgiveness wasn't about condoning the hurtful behavior, but about releasing the grip of anger and resentment that held me captive. It was a gradual process, a slow and steady shift in my internal landscape. As I began to heal, I noticed a subtle shift in my perspective. The world felt brighter, the air felt fresher, and I began to rediscover the joy of simple pleasures. I started to rebuild trust in my relationships, to open my heart to new friendships, and to embrace the beauty of human connection.

For all those like me, and I know in general too a lot of us (since duh! we are humans) who complicate every single thing in their lives, have you wondered that if you'd have not live those experiences, if you'd have not make those people your friends or not met and come across certain awful or a couple of really good people, or have you had not made those mistakes in your life you would have made them in your upcoming stage or nearer future so now you know if one generally understands it that there isn't a way for us, as people only to know better unless we lived through it. Until and unless we come through those situations of our lives when we can't process how awfully awry everything has gone or we don't know why we were so insane to make such not-so wise decisions, we would not only be able to psyche our brain and ourselves to be cautious of diving into it again or atleast be better at making decisions for the next time.

Apart from that I feel as human beings as well, we are all so different. Everybody has a different life, everybody has a different journey, everybody makes different mistakes, different things work for different people and different things are wrong for different people. So I think as a teenager or as a person in any age too, you should know that there are all kinds of slipups that you are ready for and you can gain learnings from it and you will be coming out of it as well. Try to ease out and be a wee chilled out. You are ready to be all at it and without any kind of inhibitions too. Give it some time and always try to make plans but not over complex things as most often than not we make a rigmarole of everything and later on we jump to the conclusion that it would have been better had you simplified stuff in your head, and if it does not work out remember that it is not the end of the world and you may of course, have opportunities to fix it.

The Thrill of Discovery and the Beauty of the Everyday

While the thrill of overcoming a significant challenge, like public speaking, is undeniably exhilarating, I've come to realize that discovery isn't always about grand gestures or monumental achievements. It's often found in the quiet moments, in the simple pleasures of everyday life.

If you ever are chanced upon to notice the intricate patterns of the leaves on the trees, the gentle sway of the branches in the breeze, the distant call of a bird. The sounds of the night, the rustling leaves, and the distant murmur of the city – they all mystically combine to create a work of peace.

Truly, considering to take a break and going on a vacation that is really close to nature will prove my point. In that moment, you realize that true meaning lies not in the pursuit of external validation, but in the appreciation of the present moment, in the cultivation of gratitude for the simple joys of life. It's about finding beauty in the usual, cherishing the connections we share with others, and living with intention and purpose. It's about savoring the taste of freshly brewed coffee in the morning, the warmth of the sun on your face, the laughter of loved ones.

<u>Espousing the Journey</u>

This odyssey of learning is an ongoing process, a continuous unfolding of experiences, emotions, and insights. It's a journey of self-discovery, of embracing the unknown, and of finding meaning in both the triumphs and the setbacks.

This journey invites us to be kind to ourselves, to celebrate our successes, and to learn from our mistakes. You know the way you put so much pressure onto yourself for not making mistakes but try to ease out a little and stop being too harsh on yourself and beating yourself up just for daring to commit some mistakes. Honestly, from what I have learned over the years and with no pretense again, I genuinely believe that if a mistake has been made. its been made for reason and it could be me kind of trivializing mistakes but you know that each time you do something insane or something you later on feel a lot of remorse for...know that it's been made for a reason. Remember there is always something that you learn every time you fall flat on your face, every time you make a mistake, and every time you regret something. Having said that I have grown as a person and know that each new day you have something fresh and you should not be beating your own self up just for making mistakes. Learning from them is what matters and when you do that, you will be coming back as you revisit you past self and the old memories going, "oh my god, this was so easy why did I make it so complex in my head" and it was something that happened for a reason and you finally came out of it stronger and better. Cultivate curiosity, embrace challenges, and cherish the connections that enrich your life. Reflect on your own journey. What lessons have you learned? What challenges have you overcome? *What joys have you experienced?*

CHAPTER XIV

The Art of Living – A Breather in the Chaos

Life, as we often experience it, feels like a tangled mess of deadlines, notifications, and unspoken expectations. It's easy to get caught in the whirlwind, feeling like we're constantly running a race we can't win. I remember many instances where I spotted myself in such monotonous and trying times. I was so consumed by work and academics that I barely had time to eat, let alone breathe. Assignments flooding in even on weekends. I overthought un-happened consequences, focusing on future problems that had yet to occur. I put too much pressure on myself, feeling inadequate despite my efforts. And I did feel this absolute lousy feeling. You know it felt almost a constant, gnawing anxiety. My body began to manifest the stress – headaches, sleepless nights, a persistent tension in my shoulders. It wasn't until I felt the physical toll that I realized something had to change.

We often impose these rigid structures on ourselves, these invisible rules that dictate how we "should" be living. But why? Why do we forfeit moments of joy for the illusion of control? The truth is, life doesn't have to be this complicated. It's about choices, about reclaiming the moments that are truly ours.

Chaos in the modern world isn't just about a messy desk; it's about the constant barrage of information, the pressure to be perpetually available, the fear of missing out. It's the feeling of being pulled in a million directions, leaving us feeling drained and disconnected. The consequences are real: burnout, anxiety, strained relationships, and a profound sense of dissatisfaction.

But there's another way. It's about discovering the "art of living" – finding those pockets of joy amidst the chaos, those moments of respite that recharge our souls. It's about remembering that we are human beings, not human doings.

My journey to finding this balance wasn't easy. It started with small, intentional shifts. I began scheduling short breaks throughout my day, even if it was just five minutes. During these breaks, I would step away from my laptop, and step away from my room, try and go somewhere silent like the balcony and close my eyes, and take a few deep breaths. It sounds simple, but it was transformative. It helped me clear my mind, reduce my stress levels, and reconnect with the present moment.

One of the biggest lessons I learned was the importance of setting boundaries. It's okay to say "no" to things that don't align with your values or that will further overwhelm you. It's okay to prioritize your well-being. It's not selfish; it's essential.

A refreshing vacation to recharge your batteries, or maybe just a leisurely walk in the garden, soaking in the sights and sounds around you. It could be as simple as having tea with family, letting the conversation flow freely, or losing yourself in a piece of music that makes your heart sing. Even working out can be a joyful escape, a moment to celebrate your body's capabilities, or diving into a good book—nothing beats that therapeutic feeling of getting lost in a different world.

Think about it this way: our thoughts can get tangled like the wires of our earphones. There's a certain satisfaction in untangling those knots, right? Just like that, life can get messy and heated, especially when we overuse ourselves without giving any thought to relaxation. It deserves a little fun—more than just sometimes!

It's worth noting that your body is your vehicle; it carries you everywhere, providing the means to function and enjoy every moment. Show it some respect! Treat it well, nourish it with experiences that bring you joy, and take moments to revel in these ephemeral moments. They're here one second and gone the next, so why not paint the towns red and have a blast while you can?

Now, don't get me wrong—there's nothing inherently wrong with being productive. In fact, it's essential to discern when it's time to put in the effort and strive to work hard to achieve our goals and when we might be crossing that fine line into overwhelm. Think of it as a buffet instead of a five-course meal—wouldn't you rather savor a few amazing dishes than rush through a bunch of mediocre ones?

Mindfulness practices like meditation and breath-work can be incredibly powerful tools for finding calm amidst the chaos. Even a few minutes of focused breathing can help you ground yourself and reconnect with your inner peace. And don't underestimate the power of sleep. A well-rested body and mind are better equipped to handle the challenges of daily life.

Remember those lazy summer afternoons when the world felt like it slowed down? We didn't need a packed agenda to have a good time. As simple as laying in the grass watching clouds float by, or even just hanging out with friends doing nothing could spark more joy than a meticulously planned weekend. That's the essence of respite: taking a step back, enjoying the little things, and giving ourselves permission to unwind without the pressure of productivity hanging over our heads.

So, the next time you catch yourself spiraling into the chaos of trying to do it all, pause. Ask yourself, "What's one thing I can do today that will bring me joy?" Whether it's a walk in the park, a spontaneous dance party in your living room, or simply lounging with a good book, choose to indulge in that experience fully. Life isn't about ticking off boxes; it's about creating memories, about savoring the moments that make it beautiful. It's about reclaiming your breath, finding joy in the chaos, and choosing to live a life that truly nourishes your soul. We all deserve that, and it's within our reach.

CHAPTER XV

Words: Power They Hold

Words have a way of slipping from our tongues with ease, yet their impact lingers long after they are spoken. They can heal, they can wound, they can motivate, and they can break. There is no denying that words shape the way we experience life—both in how we communicate with others and in the way we speak to ourselves. But how often do we pause and think about the weight our words carry? How often do we consider whether we are using them to build or destroy?

The Dual Nature of Words

Words can be the strongest foundation for a relationship or the wrecking ball that shatters it to dust. A single moment of kindness—a reassuring sentence, a simple 'I believe in you'—can change the trajectory of someone's life. On the other hand, a careless comment, a sharp insult, or an assumption spoken aloud can linger in someone's mind, festering longer than we ever intended.

It's astonishing how certain words, spoken years ago, still hold the power to either comfort or haunt us. Many of us remember a compliment that made us feel seen, just as we remember the hurtful words that left scars. The real question is: what kind of impact do we want our words to leave?

The Words We Never Say

While spoken words can shape the present, unspoken words shape our regrets. How many times have we left things unsaid, only to realize later that we should have spoken up? An apology left unspoken. A thank you never expressed. An 'I miss you' buried under pride.

We often assume people know how we feel about them. We assume they understand our appreciation, our care, our love. But do they? The reality is, words give clarity to feelings. When we hold back from expressing what matters, we risk leaving gaps in our relationships. Sometimes, silence speaks volumes, but sometimes, it creates distances that need not exist.

Anger vs. Temper – When Words Turn Against Us

Anger, if harnessed correctly, can be a powerful force. It can push us to take action, to demand change, to break free from limitations. It fuels movements, drives revolutions, and often compels us to stand up for what we believe in. But anger without control—when temper takes over—leads to chaos. It turns conversations into arguments, discussions into fights, and simple misunderstandings into irreversible damage.

When we let temper dictate our words, we often say things we don't mean. Words blurted out in frustration have the ability to cut deep, sometimes deeper than physical wounds. And what's worse? They can't be taken back. The person on the receiving end may forgive, but the words remain etched in their memory.

So, what's the way out? **Pause.** Before responding in anger, take a moment. Drink water. Breathe. Count to ten. Anything that buys you time before saying something you'll regret. Because in the grand scheme of things, no argument is worth leaving someone with wounds they didn't deserve.

The Unsettling Normalization of Harsh Language

There was a time when cuss words were reserved for extreme moments and then were taken under great shame as a consequence of extreme fit. Now? The insane buffoonery of people especially young adults and teenagers have made these casual fillers in daily conversations. Swearing is often seen as a symbol of confidence or strength, yet in reality, it is anything but something to take pride in. Using harsh contentious, seriously offensive language doesn't signify wisdom or depth; instead, it often reflects a lack of emotional control and maturity.

This is one of the unpopular opinions I strongly stand by: the normalization of using excessive expletives is one of the most absurd trends of our time. It is baffling how people—especially teenagers and young adults have turned profanity into a marker of confidence, humor, and even intelligence. What was once considered crass or impolite is now paraded as "cool," as if throwing in an expletive every other word somehow adds weight to a statement. Ironically, to me, it does the opposite. It strips conversations of depth, reducing language to a mere string of overused, aggressive expressions. What's even more troubling is how people, particularly the younger generation, has made this an actual habit. I was initially astonished to witness that they aren't consciously using this set skill but habitually too are spitting out this sort of offense. Social pressure fuels this too, making those who are initially reluctant feel like outliers until they too, give in. And for what? To conform to a misguided notion that swearing makes one sound bold, unfazed, or authoritative? It's laughable, really people using words they scarcely understand, often with no regard for their meanings, as if vulgarity equates to wisdom. In reality, to me, it seems like education becomes a sheer waste.

True strength lies in articulation, in the ability to express emotions and thoughts without resorting to words that degrade. The challenge is not in swearing to prove a point, but in choosing words that command respect without needing to be harsh. In a world where people are quick to speak without thinking, choosing words with intention is a rare but powerful trait.

The Art of Choosing the Right Words

The same message can be delivered in a thousand ways, and the way we phrase things determines how they are received. There is a vast difference between saying, 'You're wrong' and 'I see your perspective, but have you considered this?'

Being honest does not mean being harsh. The truth, when spoken with understanding, is far more effective than the truth spoken with cruelty. The key is not just what we say, but *how* we say it. Tone, intent, and timing all play a crucial role in communication.

We should also remember that not everything needs to be said. Being opinionated is a great trait, but being argumentative for the sake of it? Not so much. Not every battle is worth fighting, and not every thought needs to be voiced. Wisdom lies in knowing when to speak and when to stay silent.

<u>Words in the Digital Age</u>

With social media, words travel faster than ever. A tweet, a comment, a message sent in frustration—everything is out there in an instant, and nothing ever truly disappears. We live in an era where words are no longer fleeting; they are permanent.

It's easier to be thoughtless with words online than it is in real life. There's a sense of detachment, a screen that shields us from the direct impact of our words. But the emotions on the receiving end are real. Insults, criticisms, and offhand remarks can spiral into serious consequences.

The next time we type something in the heat of the moment, it's worth asking: Would I say this to someone's face? Would I want to be remembered for this comment? If the answer is no, maybe it is best left unsaid.

<u>The Power of Self-Talk</u>

The most important conversations we have are not with others, but with ourselves. The way we speak to ourselves shapes our confidence, our self-worth, and our perception of reality. If we constantly feed ourselves negativity—'I'm not good enough,' 'I always mess things up'—we start believing it. And belief dictates action.

Instead of being our own harshest critics, why not be our own motivators? Replace self-doubt with self-encouragement. Speak to yourself the way you would speak to a friend. The words we whisper to ourselves in our lowest moments hold immense power. Make sure they are words worth listening to.

The Choice We Hold

At the end of the day, words are a choice. We decide what to say, when to say it, and how to say it. And once spoken, they are no longer in our control. They take on a life of their own, shaping relationships, influencing emotions, and leaving impressions that last far beyond the moment.

So, what kind of impact do we want our words to have? Do we want to be remembered for words that uplifted, encouraged, and inspired? Or do we want to be known for words that hurt, dismissed, or destroyed?

The beauty of language is that it offers endless possibilities. Every conversation, every interaction, every message is an opportunity. An opportunity to express love, to bring clarity, to create understanding.

So, we could and we should make the choice wisely. Let's not let relationships crumble over thoughtless words. Let's ensure that the words we leave behind are ones we are proud of.

Because in the end, the power of words is not just in what they mean, but in how they make people feel. And that is something worth thinking about every time we speak.

CHAPTER XVI

Securing Satisfaction through Gratitude

Gratitude is often spoken about but rarely understood in its full depth. It's easy to say "thank you" out of habit, but do we truly feel thankful? It's preposterous, really we all have been attuned to use words we hardly understand, yet so few of us frankly reflect on the meaning behind them. Gratitude isn't just a feel-good sentiment; it's a fundamental shift in how we perceive our lives.

For a long time, I didn't pay much attention to it either. But once I made it a conscious habit—through journaling, affirmations, and simply acknowledging the good in my life, I have come to realize how much I had been taking for granted. And that's exactly what I want to come across with. Understanding how gratitude secures satisfaction in life, not through wishful thinking, but by allowing ourselves to see the plenty we already have.

The Overlooked Privilege in Everyday Life

It's human nature to focus on what's missing. We complain about what we lack, what didn't go our way, and what could have been better. But what about everything that is already good? What about the simple fact that we have access to clean water, food, shelter, and a good education? What about the people who love us, the comfort of a warm bed, or even the mere ability to wake up every morning?

The tragedy isn't that we don't have enough; it's that we fail to recognize what we do have. We operate in a world of abundance, yet we often convince ourselves of a torment born from the copious inconveniences like when the cab comes six minutes late, or the sandwich doesn't have the extra mayonnaise you asked for or you do not get to eat the favorite meal tonight. God! The scarcity we are living in? It's almost absurd how people fail to see the privileges surrounding them simply because they've become attuned to them. And that's where gratitude steps in. It reminds us that just because something is always there, doesn't mean it's any less valuable.

The Emotional Impact of Gratitude

Gratitude isn't just about listing things you're thankful for—it's about rewiring your mindset to focus on what truly matters. When you cultivate gratitude, you naturally become more emotionally resilient. You stop overanalyzing minor inconveniences and start appreciating the little joys.

Think about it: have you ever met someone who seems genuinely content no matter what life throws at them? They aren't necessarily the wealthiest, the most successful, or the ones with a perfect life. But they carry a sense of peace because they've learned to appreciate what they have rather than obsess over what they don't. Gratitude fosters this emotional balance. It acts as a buffer against dissatisfaction, disappointment, and negativity. The more you practice it, the more you realize that satisfaction isn't about having all luxuries, but it's about recognizing that you already have enough.

A Gratitude Practice – Journaling, Affirmations, and Acknowledging the Small Things

When I first started writing down the things I was grateful for, I thought it would be a short list. But as I went on, the pages kept filling up. My hand hurt, yet I still had more to write. I realized how much I had overlooked: the security of my home, the freedom to make choices, the moments of laughter with my family, the simplest pleasures like a cup of tea on a cold day.

Gratitude journaling is one of the easiest ways to shift your perspective. If you're new to it, start with just three things a day. Irregardless of them being big or small. Maybe today, you're grateful for the morning sunlight, a call with your friend, or a meal that satisfied you. The more you do this, the more you train your brain to look for the good in every situation.

Affirmations work similarly. When you affirm gratitude, you reinforce a positive outlook. Simple phrases like "I am grateful for this day," "I appreciate the people in my life," or "I choose to focus on abundance" can set the tone for your entire day. The key is consistency.

The Red and Blue Theory – Focusing on What's Right

My sister once introduced me to a well-known exercise: someone tells you to look around a room and memorize all the red objects. Then, you close your eyes, and they ask you to list the blue ones. But you can't, because you were so focused on the red that you never even noticed the blue.

This is exactly how our minds work. If you constantly focus on what's lacking, that's all you'll see. But if you train yourself to look for the good, you'll start noticing it everywhere. Gratitude is the shift from focusing on what's missing to acknowledging what's present. It's not about ignoring problems, but about achieving a balanced perspective—one that recognizes both challenges and blessings.

How Gratitude Transforms Satisfaction

We often think satisfaction comes from getting more—more success, more money, and more recognition. But real satisfaction is about shifting our mindset, not increasing our possessions. When we constantly chase the next big thing, we miss out on what's right in front of us.

Gratitude allows us to slow down and appreciate life as it is. It stops the endless cycle of "I'll be happy when..." and replaces it with "I am happy now." Once you embrace this, you stop seeing happiness as a distant goal and start experiencing it in the present.

Gratitude and Its Role in Overcoming Adversity

It's easy to be grateful when life is going well, but what about when it isn't? The truth is, gratitude isn't just about acknowledging the good—it's also about finding meaning in struggles.

Difficult times test us, but they also shape us. Looking back, some of the hardest moments in life may have been the ones that taught us the most. Gratitude helps us reframe adversity—not by sugarcoating it, but by allowing us to recognize growth, strength, and hidden blessings within challenges.

It is a Choice, Not An Order

At the end of the day, gratitude, at its core, is a very choice. A mindset. A habit. It's something that needs to be nurtured, practiced, and reinforced. The more you focus on it, the more you see its impact.

When you choose gratitude, you choose satisfaction. You choose to see the magic in ordinary moments. You choose to stop running after what's next and start appreciating what's now. And in doing so, you transform your entire life.

You Could Start Now

Here's a simple challenge: for the next seven days, write down three things you're grateful for every night. They don't have to be big—just anything that made your day better. By the end of the week, see if your perspective has shifted. You might be surprised by how much light there already is in your life.

And remember: gratitude doesn't change what you have, except it changes how you see it. And sometimes, that's all you need to secure contentment.

CHAPTER XVII

Extraordinary Within the Ordinary

Strange, isn't it, how often we convince ourselves that our world is the most chaotic, our struggles the most complex, and our thoughts the most burdened? For ourselves. Yes, life may feel like an endless storm, with our minds racing to make sense of it all. But isn't this chaos simply our own perspective, amplified by the stories we tell ourselves. It's easy to forget that others, too, are weathering their own storms — perhaps quieter, perhaps louder, but just as real.

There's a term for this realization: *sonder*. The moment you recognize that every person around you has a life as intricate and unpredictable as your own. It's like suddenly noticing that the faces in a crowded street aren't just strangers — they are protagonists in their own stories, with memories, worries, and dreams you'll never fully grasp. It's a humbling thought, one that often arrives hand-in-hand with maturity. Try someday, to not meet or have conversations but simply observe an array of personalities bustling in their own vortex. Trust me, no amount of lessons will help you gain perspective as sturdy as this will do.

Growing up isn't just about adding years to your age; it's about learning to see beyond your own narrative. We all tend to overestimate the size of our problems because we live with them every day. A heated argument, a setback, or a difficult conversation can feel monumental because our minds keep replaying it like a looping tape.   I have been the victim of its consequential endless overthinking and art of stressing out to a fault. Yet, if we step back and see our lives in the bigger picture, we realize that so much of what we carry is heightened by our thoughts. Often, the weight is less about reality and more about the stories we tell ourselves.

But this doesn't mean life isn't complex. Each of us is juggling emotions, expectations, and uncertainties. It's just that while we dwell on our struggles, we forget others are doing the same. The friend who seems carefree may be battling self-doubt. The classmate who always cracks jokes might be masking insecurities. Though every muddle is distinct, it's rare to find a journey unmarred by a topsy-turvy maze. Realizing this softens our view of others, replacing judgment with empathy.

Equally important is understanding how we anchor ourselves in things that seem important but often aren't. The material world feeds this illusion. There's a strange comfort in collecting things — better clothes, faster gadgets, fancier belongings — as if piling these up will somehow give life greater meaning. Yet these things, no matter how grand, will ultimately gather dust. They won't hold the warmth of memories or carry the strength of meaningful rapports.

It's not that having nice things is wrong; it's that chasing them with the belief they define success is where the trap lies. The truth is, fulfillment comes less from what we possess and more from the perspective we develop. A person rich in understanding carries a wealth that no possession can match.

Purpose isn't found in accumulating trophies or counting achievements. It's about being true to oneself. The world often pushes us to wear masks — to appear stronger, smarter, or happier than we feel. But deceiving ourselves with false impressions only leaves us feeling hollow. Real growth happens when we stop pretending and begin embracing what we truly value.

Staying authentic means knowing what drives you — and having the courage to follow it. For some, purpose lies in creativity; for others, it's about nurturing relationships or making a positive impact. But whatever it may be, the key is to align actions with beliefs rather than chasing illusions that impress others but betray oneself.

Curiously, the mind can be both our greatest guide and our biggest trickster. It often convinces us that we need to achieve more, own more, or become more to feel worthy. But in truth, the most extraordinary moments in life are often born from the simplest of experiences: a heartfelt conversation, a quiet evening with family, or the sense of calm found while watching the sky change colors at sunset. When you are living these moments you make no sense out of it and how amazing it is. But, after a certain time when you look back at these very moment, it aches to not being able to go back in time and just be there once again. You don't clock it. Not then atleast about the same places which never were in fact the so astounding, it was always that elusive feeling.

There's power in recognizing this. The ordinary isn't always ordinary — sometimes, it's just disguised as routine. The laughter shared over a regular daily dinner, the warmth of a quality time spent with the ones you call your home, or even the silence that lets us gather our thoughts — these are the moments that define our journey more deeply than the hoity-toity ever could.

Perspective is what makes these moments stand out. When we learn to pause, to notice what's happening beyond our own thoughts, we begin to see life differently. It's like adjusting the focus on a camera — the more we sharpen the image, the clearer we see what truly matters.

So how does one shift that focus? Curiosity is a good place to start. Ask questions — not just to others, but to yourself. Why does this feel overwhelming? Is this truly as serious as my mind is making it? What could I learn by looking at this from another angle? The more we reflect, the more we break free from the mental loops that cloud our judgment.

Equally vital is letting go of the pressure to have it all figured out. Life isn't a neatly written script; it's unpredictable, and sometimes the best moments arise when we stop controlling the narrative. Embracing uncertainty doesn't mean giving up — it means trusting that growth happens not only in clarity but also in confusion.

In the end, what leaves a lasting impact isn't what we own, but what we offer i.e. willingness to understand. This of the many qualities is what lingers in people's memories long after material possessions fade away.

So here's a thought: Perhaps living extraordinarily isn't about grand achievements or flawless plans. Maybe it's about finding perspective from the messy, unpredictability. The one where simplicity meets depth, and ordinary moments become extraordinary simply because we choose to see them that way.

Every so often, the most extraordinary moments unfold when we stop fixating on the complexities we create in our minds and start acknowledging the lesser extraordinary, the simplicity of what's real.

CHAPTER XVIII

Imperfectly Perfect

Funny how we're always reaching for something or the other to fix, to improve, to perfect. As if life should come neatly packaged with no rough edges? I mean, we scroll through feeds filled with curated perfection, chasing after an ideal that, let's be honest, doesn't really exist. We're all a bit of a mess, aren't we? And maybe, just maybe, that's where the magic lies.

Let's talk about us, the humans. We're beautifully, wonderfully imperfect. We stumble over words during presentations, replay awkward moments in our heads for hours, and sometimes, we just spill coffee on our favorite shirt. It's those little quirks, those tiny flaws, that make us, well, us. Remember that time you tried to perform a task and it came out looking like a science experiment gone wrong? Or when you said the wrong thing at the absolute worst moment? Those moments, while cringe-worthy at the time, become the stories we tell, the memories that stick. Not that I am covering the foot in the mouth side of myself but still don't these incidences add texture to our lives, a kind of depth that a perfectly smooth surface just can't offer.

We're not designed to be flawless. Know what, scrap this word off only, we're all wonderfully 'flawsome', right? Each of us, with our own twists. Our mistakes, our stumbles, they're not detours; they're part of the journey. They're the lessons we learn, the growth we experience. It's through these little cracks that the light gets in, right? It's where we find meaning. Imagine if we were all perfect. Life would be terribly boring, wouldn't it? It's in the mess, in the chaos, that we find our true selves. Accepting our flaws, turning them into strengths—that's where the real power lies.

Life, too, is never hunky-dory. It's full of ups and downs, moments of triumph and times of failure, the highs and lows that we all must navigate. But what if these vicissitudes—the challenges and changes—are part of what makes life so precious? The unpredictability of life often forces us to grow and adapt in ways we never expected. And in those moments, we must learn to cope, to breathe, and to embrace the imperfect nature of the journey.

As we go through life, it's essential to understand that there is no one top-drawer answer to the problems we face. For example, take the famous metaphor of the glass: is it half-empty or half-full? The answer depends entirely on our perspective. If you're thirsty, the amount in the glass doesn't matter as much as whether it quenches your thirst. Similarly, the meaning of life's challenges isn't dictated by their appearance, but by the way we choose to view and respond to them. It's about perspective.

We spend so much time trying to control everything, to have all the answers. But sometimes, the best thing to do is loosen your grip—to let life breathe on its own and surprise you. "The heart knows reasons that reason knows nothing of," as the saying goes. Sometimes, we don't need to rationalize everything. Sometimes, we just need to trust our gut, to go with the flow, and to surrender to the unknown.

There's a certain beauty in surrendering, in accepting that life doesn't have to be perfect to be worthwhile. It's like watching a sunset; it's never the same, but it's always breathtaking. It's in those moments of letting go that we find peace, a sense of calm amidst the chaos.

We aren't meant to be immaculate, nor is life. Yet somehow, in the rough edges and quiet chaos, things still find a way to make sense—imperfectly perfect, just as they are. The days that challenge us, the flaws that make us who we are, the perspectives that shape our world—they're all part of the puzzle. And through it all, we discover that it's not perfection we need, but acceptance and love for the beautiful mess that is life and self.

It's often easy to be caught up in the pursuit of perfection, chasing after an ideal that doesn't truly exist. So, accept them, your stumbles, your messy moments. You can eventually learn and be better the next. Embrace the unpredictability of life, the unexpected twists and turns. And remember, it's not about erasing your imperfections; it's about celebrating them. It's about acceptance, not chasing trends but authenticity, finding strength in the missteps, and joy in the journey. As face it, it's not about being perfect; it's about being real. It's about being imperfectly, wonderfully, you.

CHAPTER XIX

Parents—One of God's Greatest Gifts

Selfless and *genuine*—two words that barely scratch the surface when it comes to describing the value of the most amazing people in our lives: our parents. The role of a parent can never truly be captured in text. Their love and sacrifice transcend anything words could ever convey.

Our parents are a constant source of support and warmth. Mom and Dad aren't just figures in the background; they are the reason we're here and the foundation upon which we've built our lives. From the moment we're born, they guide us, nurture us, and think about us constantly—even when we don't realize it.

Our parents are the architects of our beginnings. From the moment we enter this world, they are our guides, our protectors, our constant companions. My own memories are filled with moments of my mother's unwavering care, her unconditional love forming the bedrock of my childhood. Even the seemingly ordinary moments, like her managing everything with effortless grace, felt extraordinary. I remember how she'd always make sure I had my favorite snack after school, no matter how busy she was. It was her way of showing she was thinking of me, even when I wasn't around. The bond I share with her is nothing like with someone else. She'll forever be the person whom I have the best rapport with.

My father's influence, though quieter, was equally profound. He instilled in me a sense of resilience, a readiness for the challenges ahead. His "hard-hitting arguments," as I used to perceive them, were actually lessons in critical thinking and preparation for the real world. We do have our own share of quibbles, and I used to get pissed off by his words a couple of times back when I was small. At the time, I felt frustrated, but now I understand he was trying to equip me for life's journey, a legacy full of insights.

My sister too, has been a pillar of support, much like my father, she's too always given me and my brother unfiltered forthright statements so to speak, often accompanied by an eye roll and a sigh. There were times I resented her honesty, particularly when it pointed out my glaringly obvious mistakes. But I've come to appreciate the value of having someone who tells you the truth, even when it hurts. I'm always appreciative of her way of dealing with things and am highly motivated by it, though I'm fairly certain she thinks otherwise but now she knows if she's reading this, actually if she's miraculously stumbled upon this, which, knowing her, is unlikely.

In today's fast-paced, digitally driven world, a concerning trend has emerged: a diminished appreciation for the tireless efforts of parents. With a constant barrage of social media comparisons and the illusion of instant gratification, many young people seem to overlook the sacrifices and unwavering support their parents provide. The focus often shifts towards material possessions or fleeting online validation, overshadowing the invaluable lessons, emotional guidance, and unconditional love that parents offer. This growing disconnect can lead to strained relationships and a profound sense of ingratitude, as the very foundation of familial support is taken for granted. It's a sobering reminder that the true measure of wealth lies not in what we accumulate, but in the appreciation we show for the people who have shaped us.

Speaking for myself, I can't even begin to express the profound gratitude I have for my lovely parents and the joy they bring to my life. They're not just the ones who brought us into this world; they're the ones whose smiles wring my heart with pure, undeniable joy. In hindsight, I find myself longing for those simple moments—holding my dad's finger as we walked, or sitting with my mom while she cooked, chatting endlessly about my day. My dad always gave me those hard-hitting reality checks, and though I might not have always paid close attention back then, in retrospect, those were golden lessons. Parents are those rock-solid cheerleaders in our lives, always there to lift us up and keep us going. In a world where fake friends can pop up like weeds, it's nice to know that our parents are the real deal—always standing by our side, no matter what.

And yet, amidst all that they do, how often do we pause to simply be with them? Have you ever wondered how much they still worry about us? Are we alright? Did we have a proper meal? Did we get home safe? Their entire world revolves around us, and sometimes all they want is to share a simple meal together or hear about our day. That's all it takes to light up their hearts.

Now, let me say this: parents may not always be perfect. They're human, just like the rest of us. There will be times when they make mistakes, and that's okay. It's important to express ourselves and share our thoughts with them when things go awry, but let's also remember to treat them with the respect they deserve. Just as we have our off days, they're entitled to be themselves, to make mistakes, and to enjoy their lives without judgment.

In the end, parents ask for so little yet give so much. So, let's give them the love and attention they've always given us. After all, we only get one set of parents—and they're one of life's greatest gifts.

CHAPTER XX

The Final Piece

Goodness! This has truly been an exhilarating odyssey. My hope is that reading these words has kindled something within you, much as writing them has done in me. As we near the end of our journey together, let me toss one final thought your way. Life—it's never as simple as we make it. As we reach the end of this little journey together, let me leave you with something to ruminate about. Life, as we know it, is never just one thing—it's a mix of so many moments, emotions, and experiences. And if you're like most of us, you've probably been tempted to box it all in, make sense of it with neat labels and definitions. What if perhaps, we stopped trying to figure everything out and instead, leaned into what life is really offering?

Why not let all emotions come and go as they please? Absorb them, reflect on them, but don't let one feeling take over. It's this calmness that brings clarity, even in the bedlam. Especially those moments when you're perturbed in life you want to just let go of the feeling, so what I suggest you to do for the last time is to not be afraid of your inhibitions at that instant, you know try and surrender to the reality because as and when you become elusive to it, then it's all the more challenging to dealing with it so learn to accept truth. Since, the more you avoid it, the harder it becomes to deal with. Allow yourself to experience life in its entirety—the joy, the uncertainty, the pain—there's a certain tranquility that follows.

I know, it's easy to be wanting to escape sometimes, to evade those tough feelings or unsettling situations. But you'll find that peace comes when you don't run away from it all. There'll be times you feel tempted to throw yourself into everything, but remember, there's a calm power in restraint. And trust me, letting it out—be it through ranting to someone who gets you, or even just crying when you need to—isn't a sign of weakness. Heck, if you can't cry freely, how will you ever smile fully?

Don't get caught up in the narrow boxes that the so called "wise" build for you. Who decided boys can't cry or girls can't be strong enough? One is worthy to be considered wise if they know for the fact that even when it comes to taking pain, women have way more ability to endure it, as you might've had heard that the pain a mother goes through whilst delivering a baby is equivalent to the excruciating pain one feels when nearly twenty bones of the body get fractured all at the same time. Cerebrally too, both men and women are on equal footing as face it; this is what feminism really is all about, not the overblown or misunderstood version people often scoff at. Plus, isn't emotional strength about knowing when and to whom to open up? That, my friend, is what life is—finding that **balance**. And it's in that very act of finding balance, of defying those narrow boxes that we begin to truly live life on our own terms.

Living life on your own terms. The phrase itself carries a certain allure, a sense of liberation from the should's and ought to's that often dictate our choices. It's not about rebellion for the sake of it, but about reclaiming authorship of our own narratives.

In a world that often tries to fit us into pre-defined boxes, living on our own terms is an act of defiance, a declaration that we will not be confined by someone else's expectations. It's about recognizing that our lives are not scripts to be followed, but canvases to be painted with our own unique colors.

This isn't about ignoring the world around us, but about filtering it through our own values, our own aspirations. It's about discerning what truly matters to us, and having the courage to pursue it, even when it diverges from the well-trodden path.

Living on your own terms means questioning the status quo, challenging the assumptions that hold us back. It's about asking ourselves: "What do I truly want? What brings me joy? What kind of life do I want to create?"

It's also about understanding that this journey is not a solitary one. We are not islands, and our choices inevitably impact those around us. But it's about navigating those relationships with authenticity, with a clear sense of our own boundaries and values.

This approach requires us to be adaptable, to embrace the unexpected turns in the road. It asks us to be honest with ourselves, to acknowledge our limitations, and to celebrate our strengths. It's about being comfortable with imperfection, with the knowledge that we are all works in progress.

And it's important to remember that living on your own terms doesn't mean a life devoid of challenges. In fact, it often means facing them head-on, with a sense of purpose and resilience. It's about navigating the inevitable setbacks and disappointments with grace, knowing that they are part of the journey.

Ultimately, living life on your own terms is about creating a life that is authentic, meaningful, and fulfilling. It's about aligning our actions with our values, our passions, our dreams. It's about choosing to write our own story, rather than letting someone else write it for us. And that, my friend, is a journey worth taking.

It's also essential to make a mention of an ever pressing conundrum that keeps knocking on the doors of our minds: How do we truly stumble upon the opportunities that matter? Or to make it simple: *How do we find good opportunities?* It's one of those riddles that seems to follow us through life, isn't it? In my reckoning, the answer lies not in waiting for the perfect moment but in actively creating it. Opportunities, I believe, are like seeds waiting for the right conditions to grow. And the most fertile ground? A proactive self-analyzer—someone unafraid to confront their flaws and openly discuss them with those you trust the most. That inner circle, your most honest layer of people, can offer insights and support that sharpen your perspective.

But self-awareness is just the beginning. Life doesn't hand over its treasures to the faint-hearted. It demands that we persevere through setbacks, adapt to mismatches, and remain calm when the horizon seems uncertain. Boldness and thoughtfulness must go hand in hand. Stay calm, take calculated risks, and prepare yourself mentally for both success and failure. One often requires a sagacious mind, one willing to rationalize, adapt, and see potential where others may not.

Opportunities aren't wrapped in ribbons; they're ordinarily hidden behind challenges, requiring a mind willing to think, adapt, and persist. And here lies life's quiet wisdom: balance courage with rationality, boldness with patience. Be curious, be open, and trust that the best opportunities aren't merely stumbled upon—they're crafted by those who dare to imagine them into existence.

At long last, I'm just someone who has picked up a few things along the way, trying to share what I've learned with you. Major props go to my parents, who've been the most enlightening people in every respect. I deeply revere and respect my religion for its absolutely enriching and invigorating insights. Oddly enough, there's no secret formula no one-size-fits-all answer. You see, life's a bit like one of those jigsaw puzzles we used to do as kids. As you close this book, I invite you to consider one small step you can take today to embrace the 'unfinished puzzle' of your own life.

You've got pieces scattered everywhere—some are obvious, while others take a bit more effort to figure out. Throughout this voyage, people—whether they're therapists, parents, or loved ones—may help you find the missing pieces. They might even guide you in putting them together just as I've endeavored to do through this book, aiming to help you in getting a hold of a lost piece or two as well. But here's the thing: **only you**—and no one else—can complete that puzzle.

As far as life is concerned, so to speak, for each to their own is the answer to *"What's life, is it?"*

Acknowledgements

Well, folks, here we are! This whole "writing a book" thing... honestly, it was a bit of a madcap idea. If you had told me a while back that I'd actually go through with it, I probably would have choked on my tea. So, first off, a massive thank you to you, the readers, for joining me on this wonderfully irrational journey. Who knew anyone besides me would be up for reading this piece?

First and foremost, all gratitude to the Almighty for bestowing upon me this beautiful, albeit sometimes chaotic, life—as beautiful as it could ever be—and for giving me the ability to translate my thoughts down into words.

Major props to my parents, my ever-shining beacons of light and guidance: you've weathered every storm with me, and for that, I am eternally grateful. Thanks for not disowning me during my more... "expressive" teenage years.

Ahem, now for the siblings. To that motley crew of (sometimes) helpful advice-givers, thank you for the insights, even if they were delivered with a healthy dose of sibling rivalry. Life wouldn't be quite as colorful without you lot. To my amazing teachers back in school, from whom I learned a lot even if I might not have fully understood it all back then. I am immensely grateful to all of you!

And finally, to this incredible, perplexing, beautiful thing we call life. This book is dedicated to you. Thanks for all the ups, the downs, and the 'what on earth was that?' moments. And to you, dear reader, whether you've skimmed a bit or devoured every word, thank you so much for joining me.

Well, this is where I wave goodbye. I'll let you get back to your life. Thank you again for taking a chance on this book—it means the world! Now, if you'll excuse me, I'm off to celebrate with a cup of tea and the satisfaction of finally finishing this thing. Wish me luck!

About The Author

Aamir Raza began writing 'Life, is it?' at the age of fourteen, mostly as a way to put scattered thoughts about life into words.Two years later, at sixteen, those reflections became his first published book.

He is currently a student with a strong interest in reading, writing, and spoken expression. Over the years, he has been drawn to different forms of storytelling and communication, from early theatre experiences to public speaking and exploring both written and spoken art.

Much of Aamir's writing comes from simple observations of everyday life and the questions that quietly sit behind them. 'Life, is it?' is his attempt to share those reflections in a way that feels honest, leaving them open for readers to interpret in their own way and perhaps return to whenever they instinctively seek comfort or a quiet place to confide in.

9 798889 840968